THE WHITE CROSS LIBRARY.

YOUR FORCES, AND HOW TO USE THEM.

BY
PRENTICE MULFORD.

VOL. III.

NEW YORK CITY:
F. J. NEEDHAM,
1895

Copyright, 1889,
By F. J. NEEDHAM.

CONTENTS.

The practical use of reverie.

Your two memories.

Self teaching; or the art of learning how to learn.

How to push your business.

The religion of the drama.

The uses of sickness.

Who are our relations?

The use of a room.

Man and wife.

Cure for alcoholic intemperance.

The mystery of sleep, or our double existence.

The church of silent demand.

GOD.

A Supreme Power and Wisdom governs the Universe. The Supreme Mind is measureless, and pervades endless space. The Supreme Wisdom, Power and Intelligence is in everything that exists from the atom to the planet.

The Supreme Power and Wisdom is more than *in* everything. The Supreme Mind *is* everything. The Supreme Mind is every atom of the mountain, the sea, the tree, the bird, the animal, the man, the woman. The Supreme Wisdom cannot be understood by man or by beings superior to man. But man will gladly receive the Supreme thought and wisdom, and let it work for happiness through him, caring not to fathom its mystery.

The Supreme Power has us in its charge, as it has the suns and endless systems of worlds in space. As we grow more to recognize this sublime and exhaustless wisdom, we shall learn more and more to demand that wisdom draw it to ourselves, make it a part of ourselves, and thereby be ever making ourselves newer and newer. This means ever perfecting health, greater and greater power to enjoy all that exists, gradual transition into a higher state of being and the development of powers we do not now realize as belonging to us.

We are the limited yet ever growing parts and expressions of the Supreme Never Ending Whole. It is the destiny of all in time to see their relation to the Supreme and also to see that the straight and narrow path to ever-increasing happiness is a perfect trust and dependence on the Supreme for the all round symmetrical wisdom and idea which we individually cannot originate. Let us then daily demand faith, for faith is power to believe and power to see that all things are parts of the Infinite Spirit of God, that all things have good or God in them, and that all things when recognized by us as parts of God must work for our good.

That cry for "rest for the soul," or "rest of the spirit," which goes up unheard from thousands today, and which involves at times a weariness and even disgust for life, comes entirely of weariness of mind, and consequent weariness of body, through mental habits and states of mind unconsciously formed, leading to exhaustion and depletion of life's forces; and such exhaustion and depletion are the causes of disease, inability to enjoy life or attain success in life. Mental or spiritual force here means that literal, unseen element, your thought, which, as you send from you and concentrate and direct on persons far or near, can "push things" and accomplish results, though the persons acted on be a thousand or ten thousand miles distant from your body. This force you can constantly increase, by means which to some may seem very trivial.

THE PRACTICAL USE OF REVERIE.

COPYRIGHTED, 1888, BY F. J. NEEDHAM.

You do not need to be thinking all the time during your waking hours. Such habit of mind soon exhausts, and keeps you putting out the same set of thoughts, a train of idea over and over again.

One of the greatest sources of power and health, both of mind and body, is the ability to dismiss all positive thought at will, to sit perfectly quiet physically, to pass, if but for a few seconds, into a dreamy state or reverie; to see only the landscape that may be before the physical eye, or even but a very small part of that, or to allow the mind to dwell and **live** in such mental pictures as may come to it.

Strength is born of Rest.

In such manner and by such process, perhaps unconsciously practised, does the painter seize upon some choice bit of scenery, separating and cutting it, as it were, from the rest, and transferring it to canvas. You may have many a time passed it by without really seeing it as he depicts it, because your mind was roaming or working hither and thither in every direction, one second being in your home, the next at your store, shop, or office, then wrestling with a difficulty, then worrying over a trouble, and, in fact, engaged with more things in sixty seconds than you could write out in one hour. All this is work. It is expenditure of force. It is very often a useless expenditure of force. It brings no clear, no new idea. It is exactly as if the woodman spent two hours in wildly brandishing his axe before he set to work cutting down the tree.

Sixty seconds of reverie or meditation are sixty seconds of actual rest to mind and body.

Even on the lower partial plane of success, that of mere money accumulation, it is the man who can control a few moments of reverie at will, or, in other words, the man who can dismiss his thought when he pleases, and thereby rest his mind for ever so few moments; it is he who holds the reins of financial power, for it is during these moods of rest, or reverie, that the door is opened for new, fresh ideas, and it is the new idea plan device first, and the persistent silent force to hold these in mind, and *in that way* push them afterward, that coins money.

Have you much capacity for seeing anything, or

even enjoying what you do see, when you are on the run? You may then pass by and fail to notice the person whom of all others you most desire to see, and whom it may be most profitable for you to see. Bank bills may then lie in your path unnoticed.

In mental condition, thousands of people about us are breathless, hurried, and on the "dead run," and running from year to year in the same rut of thought. They cannot, in such mental condition, see opportunities for pushing their fortunes. They have not the courage to take hold of opportunities if they do see them. They do today exactly what they did yesterday, and do that *only* because they did it yesterday. They are the slaves, not of the capitalist or monopolist, but of their own mental condition, which binds them to continual and monotonous ruts of thought and consequent action, by chains stronger than any of iron. They have no ability for bringing themselves into these desirable states of mental rest. They think they must be doing something with mind or body all the time. Their minds work in the same direction when their bodies are in the unconscious state called sleep. Their sleep brings them, on the body's waking, not one-half the refreshment or strength as will come to those who cultivate periods of reverie, mental abstraction, or meditation, call it as you may.

While traveling on the steamboat, these never-rest-me people will wander continually through the cabins, and from one end of the boat to the other,

Strength is born of Rest.

without aim or object, looking for they know not what. On the railway train they have but one impatient desire, to get to their place of destination as soon as possible, and when there arrived, may not know what to do with themselves. In their households they are always "pottering about," working the body a great deal, and at the day's end, as regards any real advancement of fortune or business, have accomplished next to nothing.

All this is keeping up a mental tension, an outlay of actual force, and for what? It is keeping the violin string stretched to its utmost tension when the instrument is not in use. It is keeping the engine running when there is no work to do, no machinery to move. It is an inevitable source of exhaustion, disease, and weakening of the body.

Gen. Grant's cigar won for him more victories than his sword, for without any regard to the action of tobacco on the organization, the mere act of its inhalation, the puffing forth again and the almost unconscious watching of the smoke curls, causes, if but for ever so few seconds, the condition of reverie or mental abstraction which brings the mind into the negative or receptive condition, and in such condition it can not only rest, but receive new ideas. We here neither recommend nor condemn tobacco, but speak of it only as an imperfect agency, when so used, for inducing that certain mental state which helped Grant temporarily to hold his mental forces in reserve, and act to advantage when occasion required.

Strength is born of Rest.

The same mental state can be brought by other and more natural means, and, as these are cultivated, the results will be far more profitable and lasting.

Such as these: Stop here, and now as you read this page throw yourself back in your chair, let your arms hang passive on the chair arms or on your lap, and think of nothing, if but for three or five seconds. If a cloud in the sky, or a curl of vapor, or a tree branch moved by the wind arrest your eye, look on them so long as they amuse you and no longer. If you cannot cease working with mind or body even for five seconds (and a great many people cannot), cease your abrupt, spasmodic, physical motions. If you must move your arm, do so, if but once, as slowly as possible. You have now taken your first exercise in the cultivation of reverie or mental abstraction. You have given yourself an atom of real rest. You have drawn to your mind an atom of power which you will never lose. You cannot expect immediate success in the cultivation of this much needed faculty. You may have the hurried mental habit of a whole lifetime gradually to overcome. But the seed of repose is now sown within you. This thought will never leave you. Don't try too hard to cultivate it. Let it come up and grow of itself, as it assuredly will.

You can carry this mental discipline or control of body into the most trivial acts (so erroneously called) of every-day life, as when you rise up or **sit** down, or in turning the pages of a book, or **turn** over your newspaper, or in opening a door or **win-**

Strength is born of Rest.

dow. For when you perform any of these acts in an impatient, jerky, spasmodic fashion, regarding them as irksome barriers betwixt you and something you wish to arrive at, you expend a great volume of force unnecessarily. You can expend force enough in the impatient turning of the leaves of this book to do a half hour's composed, careful work; and the finer your mind, the more varied and fertile your thought, the greater is its power, and the more of it do you through hurried act waste. When you so cultivate the reposeful mood during your waking hours, you are cultivating also the capacity for sounder and more healthful sleep, for the predominant mood of the day is the predominant mood of the night. Sleeplessness comes from lack of mental control, or the habit of never-ceasing, spasmodic, fitful thought, leading surely to spasmodic, fitful, physical acts; and if the mind cannot control the body in the daytime, and keep it in a restful and force receiving state, neither can it control the body at night. Such is the mind which may keep you for hours awake, turning and tossing, unable to sleep, until your bones and flesh ache from weariness.

But as you cultivate reverie or mental rest, your mind will grow to such power that you can induce sleep or a state of rest at any time.

Don't practise these or corresponding methods when it is irksome or frets you. If you do, you retard rather than advance. Try these methods *only* when they please you. The beauty and mys-

Strength is born of Rest.

tery of all real growth of spiritual or mental force is, that like corn or wheat, it grows when we are asleep or unconscious of such growth. Two, three, five years hence, your whole bearing, manner and physical movement will be changed into the slower, more graceful force, holding reposeful mood and action of power. The body is literally banged to pieces by the mental action and mood of unrest. Thoughts flying to no purpose and without control here, there, everywhere, and on everything, hour after hour, and day after day, do literally tear the physical machine to pieces.

Every physical act, even your steps in walking, as the mood of deliberation and repose is cultivated, can be made a source of pleasure; and when your physical movement is pleasant to you and not irksome, your work, be it what it may, is not only well done, but in the pleasant doing you are drawing more and more power to yourself, and such power comes to stay forever. This principle extends to all art, be it oratory, acting, painting, sculpture, and is the secret of superior attainment in all art and in all business; and as it is more cultivated, as in the soon coming future it surely will be, men and women will, in so increasing their power, accomplish results as incredible to the masses, at the present moment, as were the possibilities of the electric telegraph to our great-grandfathers. **The "miracle," so called, of Biblical history, was a result attained solely through this storing up and concentration of mental power.**

Strength is born of Rest.

Christ and Moses — the seers, soothsayers, and magicians of antiquity — held their minds in repose, and in so doing accumulated and held that thought power or element which, when concentrated and directed on a sick man, could fill him instantly with new life; or if acting on the elements, could bring loaves and fishes apparently out of nothing, or calm the storm, or bring water from the barren rock. When Christ commended Mary for not "cumbering herself with the never-ceasing details of household affairs, as did Martha," he implied that Mary had "chosen the better part," because, in holding herself more aloof from the cares of the house, she was gaining a power which could eventually do far more in ever so few moments, when properly directed, even for home comfort, than could Martha in a day or week, with all her physical industry and bustling about.

Martha was fretting herself to death, Mary was building herself up.

Thousands of Marthas today dissipate life's forces and ruin their health in dusting trumpery, keeping the poker and tongs set at just such an angle, and rushing their tired bodies about from morning till night, from one act to another, without one second of mental rest. Thousands of male Marthas do the same thing in their lines of action.

In so cultivating and developing the capacity to hold at will long or short periods of mental abstraction or thought and force resting, you are building up and ever increasing in power and volume the un-

Strength is born of Rest.

THE PRACTICAL USE OF REVERIE.

seen element, which going from you can act on other minds far and near, and thereby effect results most favorable to your material fortunes. Yet this same power or element you can turn upon yourself with most unprofitable results, as people do who are ever on the hurry-skurry, or who are unable to rest so long as a pot-lid remains in the house unscoured, or a mote of dust is seen in a corner of the room. Neatness can degenerate into a mania, and a man or woman's whole mind and force can be expended wholly on objects within the walls of a small room, leaving nothing to work with outside.

Exercise in these short periods of mental rest or thought dismissal will increase your capacity for presence of mind. Presence of mind means the ability to call up at a moment's notice, in any emergency, all your judgment, reason, tact, decision, and fertility of idea. Presence of mind is mind not thrown off its centre. It is the impassioned actor's corner-stone. It gives the orator the word, or sentence, or idea fit for the time and place. It is the business man's protection in or out of his counting-room. Wearied mind, which has frittered itself away on uncontrolled thought, cannot summon its forces together for action on any sudden alarm or unexpected turn of affairs. The rested and reposeful mind is the rested garrison of your thought fortress.

Presence of mind is the mind holding its power through this ability to give itself rest and store up force, and is the secret of all ease and grace of

Strength is born of Rest.

physical movement. The inspired danseuse acts up to this law. So does he or she who sings or plays from the soul. So do all who really excel in any art or calling. As mind is more and more trained in this direction, it gains power for recuperation in almost imperceptible periods of time. It can be receptive or drawing in power one second, and giving it out in effort the next. In the dance, in acting, in oratory, it can absorb a new idea, a new method unlike any it has shown in any similar previous effort, and put this immediately into execution. For such reason genius, whether on the platform or the stage, rarely expresses itself twice alike. It is the secret of the successful billiard player as well as that of the superior marksman. Hurried, nervous, and consequently ever-tired people, rarely become good shots or "experts" at anything. Mind ever on the quiver puts the body also in a quiver, so that neither the gun or the cue can be held steadily. Learn to hold your force and rest your mind, and your nerves will become as strong and steady as steel. For these nerves of ours are the conveyancers and channels for carrying thought to any part of your body which it is desirable your thought should act on and through. Such training will make you the master of the most vicious and unruly horse. Such training is the foundation of courage. It is the tired mind, and consequently exhausted body, that is most open to the current of fear. The moment fear seizes upon you in holding the reins, the excited animal feels that you are afraid of him, for

---

Strength is born of Rest.

you have sent your mood of mind, or element of fear, literally into him. It was this superior force, so gained, that made the prophet Daniel keep the lions at bay, when put in their den. There is no limit to the possibilities coming of it. It can make the body superior to any material element. It is the power which caused the three young Jews, Shadrach, Meshach, and Abednego, to pass through the fiery furnace unharmed. It was the power in Paul that made the viper's sting harmless to him. This power belongs also to you. It is in you in the germ. It can make any organ or function of your organization ten times more powerful to act than at present.

Reverie, like any other faculty, can be developed to excess, as in the case of dreamy, absent-minded persons, who lose themselves in their day dreams, forget where their bodies are, or even what their bodies may be doing. They lack the positive force to awaken themselves to action when action is necessary. There is an equilibrium to be established between our positive and negative forces (the negative being reverie), so that you can throw yourself into either state at will, and at any time or place. In this way you are constantly resting, even as you work with mind or body, and so nicely can this equipoise be adjusted, that you may always receive a little more force than you expend, so keeping ever a reserve of strength, exactly as the engineer keeps a reserve of steam in the boiler. Many people now use up their steam or force as fast as they receive it, one result of which is, they fail, or fall sick, or lose

Strength is born of Rest.

their heads entirely on occasion of any unexpected or unusual strain, pressure, or emergency.

As you cultivate more and more the ability to give yourself, at any time you desire, these mental rests (presuming that your mind is always in the attitude of good will to all), your physical breathing will become slower, deeper, and more healthful and strength giving. You will then inhale and exhale air from the very bottom of the lungs, and not from or near the top, as do panting, hurried, restless, and jerky people.

All healthful changes of mind or spirit must cause corresponding healthful and beneficial changes to the body, for it is your spirit that is ever remaking or changing your body to its own likeness.

The reverse of this is sadly true, for if your mind lives in the thought of sickness, or any kind of unhealthful thought, it will fashion the body after the likeness of such thought.

But there is an inhalation or breathing of your spirit, of which that of the lungs is a coarser type, and when you are at peace with the world, and are living in the current of constructive thought, this ability for reverie or mental abstraction, if but for two or three seconds, will enable your spirit to reach up literally higher and higher, and inhale an atmosphere of element far finer, more powerful, and fuller of life than any on the earth's stratum of existence; and as through this exercise your power increases to so dismiss thought, and throw yourself into this state, you will receive and feel from such ele-

Strength is born of Rest.

ment an exhilaration and healthful buoyancy far exceeding that coming of any earthly stimulant or force. This is one means for realizing the "divine ichor" of the ancient mythology. It is one means for gaining the real "elixir of life."

It will give you a tremendous force to act with in all material or "practical affairs," when the time, place, and opportunity call for action. Thousands of people today, through the mania for ever keeping themselves on a mental tension, and of deeming themselves sick if not always strung up to that tension, do by their own acts retard instead of advance their fortunes. In their hurried mental condition, they lack tact in dealing with others. They repel instead of inviting those who could most benefit them, and, although often people of great energy, they fall far short of the position they might occupy did they give themselves more repose.

They lose also hours of time and volumes of force, in the endeavor to repair the consequences of their own hurry and imperfect effort. They "sling things" about unconsciously, lose their pencils, their penknives, mislay important letters, lose money in making change, and are always looking for something mislaid in the mood of hurry. Of what practical use is force so expended?

The mental attitude of "good will to all," above spoken of, does not imply that humble, servile, abject frame of mind which endures outrage and injury **without** resistance or protest, deeming it to be **a merit**. You may desire the best for the man who **tries to**

Strength is born of Rest.

set your house on fire, but common sense tells you to prevent him by all possible means from setting it on fire. If a fool attempts to tyrannize over you or abuse you, you will resist him. When his foolishness is put down, you can show your good will for him. When Christ cast out devils, he was neither gentle nor humble in commanding them to leave the persons they tormented.

Strength is born of Rest.

YOUR TWO MEMORIES.

COPYRIGHTED, 1888, BY F. J. NEEDHAM.

You have two memories, as you have or are composed of two selves: the physical, or temporary self, and the spiritual, or eternal self. You have an earthly memory, a perishable belonging of your temporary, physical self, and a spiritual memory, a belonging of your eternal and indestructible self.

Your earthly memory is as much a part of your physical body as any other organ of that body. Its use is the retention in mind of events on the physical stratum of existence. It is formed only to deal with material substance, even as your eye or your sense of touch can only be used for material substance. Your spirit has experiences in its spiritual realm of existence. It goes to other places, meets persons, exchanges thought, participates in enjoyments; but when it returns to the body, there is of that body no organ capable of receiving or preserving the spiritual picture, or impression, of such experiences.

The physical organ of memory is subject to decay, like the other physical organs, as is sometimes seen in cases of people with very old physical bodies. In other words, the worn-out body will have the **worn-out physical organ of memory**.

Thought is an Element.

The earthly memory need not decay, no more than the earthly body need decay. But if you have faith only in material things, and what you call material laws, your body and all its functions, memory included, must go the way of all material things — to decay. Such decay and loss of memory has happened to bright intellects, whose sundering of spirit from their body has been of comparatively recent date — men whose thoughts, at times, penetrated far into the higher world of spirit; who brought from thence live food for many minds; who have made a deep impress on our age, but who still, unfortunately, lived too far within the domain of material things and influences to escape the inevitable result to the earthly body and earthly mind of such influences, that result being the decay of the body, the physical instrument for the spirit's use on the physical stratum of life.

It must be kept in mind, as much as possible, that your body and your spirit are two distinct and separate things or factors, as the carpenter and his saw are separate things; that your spirit has used, and through ignorance, or lack of power, worn out many bodies, as the carpenter may have used and worn out many saws; and that with ever-increasing knowledge and power your spirit may, instead of wearing your body out, as heretofore, renew it ever with finer and finer material.

Your memory is an actual photographic plate, constantly taking pictures of all scenes and events palpable to the other senses, by a process of which our artificial photography is a coarse and feeble imitation.

Thought is an Element.

Of this we have a suggestion in the power of a certain kind of clairvoyance, to see through contact with a piece of rock, or coal, the pictures of the scenery and events happening about it, and imprinted on it through far distant geological periods. On all material substances, wood, or stone, or metal, are being constantly photographed the images of all material things surrounding them. The physical organ of memory is a plate still more sensitive, for which the physical eye is the outward lens. The physical organ of memory also takes and preserves the pictures of your own thoughts and those of others, as they give them to you.

If you do not crowd the plate, or hurry the process, through a hurried condition of mind, through trying to see or remember too much at once, you will get and retain of what you do see, or of what is going on about you, the clearer pictures.

You have an earthly memory, for use on the earth stratum of life, and a spiritual memory, for use on the spiritual side of your life, even as you have the spiritual correspondence, or duplicate of all your other senses, such as hearing, seeing, smelling, tasting, touching. None of the spiritual senses, save in exceptional instances, are brought into play in the earthly, or physical life.

When lives are more perfected, or ripened, on this planet, as they will be, all these senses will come into play. Then your true life begins. For all of your physical existence and all belonging to it is, **as compared with the exercise of your spiritual and finer senses,** but as a coarse shell or envelope.

Thought is an Element.

You are here in the physical, as compared with the spiritual, as is the grub, when compared with the butterfly; the full-grown oak, as compared with the acorn. But all comparisons must fall far short, in the endeavor to suggest the possibilities and powers coming to your real or spiritual life.

The "earthly memory," as here used, is but a relative term. It implies a memory filled entirely with material cares and considerations. But your memory, through aspiration and persistent desire for a more perfect life, will gradually refine from the coarser to the finer, from the earthly to the spiritual; in other words, you will hold in your memory only those things which can give you lasting power and pleasure; and, as you continue to do this, your memory will in time take hold of and retain the impression of your other, now unknown, life, your spiritual life, of which you may at first retain glimpses, during your waking moments, or physical daily existence, which glimpses may grow at last to clear and perfect recollection.

These are the possibilities, remember, of every human spirit; possibilities certainly to be realized by every spirit at some period of existence.

If you allow your mind to be continually troubled about some matter of small import, if you keep all day in memory the idea or thought that your friend may not come, as you expect, that your milliner may forget some detail in the trimming of your hat, that the mail may not bring you an expected letter, that money due you may not be paid; or if you hold in

Thought is an Element.

memory a picture of yourself as destitute or penniless, or all but penniless, next month, you are then filling your mental photographic plate entirely with pictures of the material, the perishable. So keeping memory in the material, you are making it material, and consequently subject to decay. Worse; you are keeping from memory better thought, which would give you aid and power to overcome the very things you fear.

If you overburden your memory with names and dates and events and details, you may carry a load of no use at all; and in carrying this load, you destroy capacity to receive new impressions and new ideas. The photographer wants a perfectly clear and clean plate on which to take his picture. Even so, to receive new ideas must your mental photographic plate be clear, and free of old pictures. For this reason is it, that people whose minds are full of memorized ideas and opinions, who are walking encyclopedias of facts, so called, are rarely people of original idea. They are collectors, rather than originators, and collectors, in many cases, of mental rubbish; of opinion and fact, so called, which will be found erroneous fifty years hence, even as so much of the opinion current fifty years ago seems ridiculous today.

Your successful man is often the man who, in early life, received little education. His memory was not crammed and burdened with words or opinions, which he was taught implicitly to receive as genuine. His mind was left the more free and clear

Thought is an Element.

to receive fresh impressions. For this reason, he saw the plan, the scheme, the device, the new road to success which the book-filled brain could not; for this reason, in so many cases, do uncultured, illiterate men take the lead in so many undertakings, while the man of education drudges in illiteracy's office, on small wages. When your child is able to repeat a whole dictionary "by heart," and can repeat from memory sentence on sentence, and chapter on chapter from its school-books, it is simply overloading and abusing a physical organ or function. Its real mental power is crippled. Its mental photographic plate is blurred, and crowded with old pictures, and its capacity for "getting on in the world" is lessened, instead of increased. The world calls the proper pronunciation of a word, the proper wording of a sentence, "culture." But this is not *mental power;* and to keep a memory loaded with rules, declensions, conjugations, and words, is like expending all the labor on the polishing of the knife blade, with no regard to the sharpness of its edge. Polish is a help, but not the *power* which puts you ahead in the world. A great deal is committed to memory at school which people can really give no clear reason for being learned, other than the fear of the child's being ridiculed for ignorance in after years were certain matter not learned; and of all the mass of matter memorized at school or college, two-thirds of it is fortunately forgotten within a twelve-month after being so memorized.

If you thought it a necessity to remember exactly

Thought is an Element.

how many tacks there were in your parlor carpet, and their exact distance from each other, and the number of pins in your work-box, you would have your mental photographic plate occupied with a set of useless pictures. We burden ourselves in life with hundreds of little cares, equally useless. Care and precision are valuable qualities, but if a man puts them all on his coat buttons, or a woman on the brightness of her tin pans, there is not much force left for things which may bring far more important results; and that is one reason why your man careless as to many little things, succeeds, while a very precise man may fail, or fill a smaller place in the world. Nelson, on shipboard, cared little whether the brasswork was polished to the extreme of brightness, and, as to many details, was called a slovenly commander, but he kept mind and memory very clear for the most effective method for laying his ships alongside of those of the enemy, and fighting them afterward.

Martinets have not, as a rule, won battles; not for lack of bravery, but because their memories were overcharged with the necessity for having buttons and gun-barrels in an exact line on parade, and long habit and training forced them to keep in mind these and other details, to the exclusion of the best method of obtaining the results that gun-barrels were made for.

We do not here, by any means, slight carefulness, exactness, or precision, but we do suggest **the great importance of the thing you put your care on, or what**

Thought is an Element.

you burden your memory with, or, in other words, print on your mental photographic plate. It is an organ, a function, like any other. It can be overloaded and abused, even in a good cause; and when, madam, you call to your husband, as he leaves the house to go to business in the morning, not to forget going to market, and then deliver your message to the milliner, and stop in at the store and buy the thread to match a certain shade of silk, a sample of which you have given him, you are putting extra loads on the poor man's memory, possibly already overburdened, and you will remember that the effort to remember a paper of pins, or the imprint of that paper of pins on memory's organ, makes as large a picture as the performance of some business detail necessary to secure that million.

You lose the spirit and substance of a speaker's thought when you "take notes." You do not need to retain in mind the precise words he uses. When you take notes, your mind is then necessarily diverted from the speaker. You break off, temporarily, a certain blending 'twixt his mind and yours, which makes between you a channel of mental communication and of thought absorption. You lose, also, the force and substance of what he is saying while you are writing what he has said. You are also impeding, to an extent, the speaker's flow of thought, be his discourse written or verbal, for in any case, every interested hearer is a help to the speaker, in sending him a current of sympathetic, appreciative, and responsive thought; and when you cut this off,

Thought is an Element.

you cut off a certain help and stimulation that you may have previously been sending him.

If you trust, in these cases, entirely to memory, it will more and more write down, and retain for you all of the substance, pith, and meaning of any speaker's thought, so far as you are capable of comprehending that speaker, all of which you can afterward recall to yourself, by your own method of expression.

A mental reporter, without taking notes, will sometimes give the substance of a speech in one-tenth the number of words required to deliver it in; and for practical purposes in journalism, such reporting is the most highly valued. Such a reporter trusts and cultivates what, for lack of other words, we must call his "spiritual memory"; that is, the memory which retains ideas, instead of words, for words are but vehicles to carry ideas in, and, in many cases, very imperfect vehicles.

Your spiritual memory retains the results, or wisdom gathered throughout all your past physical lives, or re-embodiments. The more numerous these lives, the older your spirit, the greater is your wisdom. In other words, the clearer then is your insight, your intuition, which means the teachings of your own spirit, which is the only teacher and source of knowledge for you in the universe.

The spiritual memory, after many re-embodiments, and with increasing power, affects, in a certain way, the physical memory; that is, the memory of the body you are now using.

Thought is an Element.

You go to a strange, possibly a foreign city you never before, in this physical life, visited. You are possessed by a strange sensation of having been there before. You may feel strangely at home among new people, scenes, and customs. That comes of the working of your spiritual memory. You have been there before in some previous physical existence. You were of these people. You lived among them, and then belonged to them.

If you are strongly drawn to, and greatly interested in some particular era of history, and have, during all your present life, read and re-read everything concerning it with the greatest relish, and every bit and scrap of new information concerning such historical era is still seized upon by you, and, in a mental sense, almost greedily devoured, it is because your spiritual memory, imperfect and clogged as it is, by the confusion and false beliefs written on your physical memory, as to your real self and the now hidden powers in that self, seizes on these historical pictures, as presented to you in story or print, and feels, rather than recognizes, your former participation in those events. This is why the history of one nation, or an era of such nation's history, may be of more interest to you than any other. You lived in that era, and acted in it. It was a period of marked impression and event in your real life. The forces, perhaps, long gathering in quiet within you, and through, possibly, a succession of quiet, and relatively uneventful, physical lives, burst forth in that era into a certain energy and fruition, and your spir-

Thought is an Element.

itual, or real self, now so far dominates your physical self as to force it to recognize its life and effort, and possibly, even its individuality, during that era. Your present physical life is but one of a series of physical lives. Your real self passes from one to another of these lives, with greater or less intervals of time between such physical lives, something as your body passes from one suit of clothes to another, as the last suit is worn out. As you increase in force and wisdom, the time between each re-embodiment becomes less and less, because your spirit, your highest self knows, or is forced through a peculiar intuition, to return to the earth stratum of life, that it may as soon as possible get the power which it can only get there; and that power once matured, it has never again to return under the slow, and generally painful conditions of a physical rebirth. That power once matured, it can return to earth at will. In other words, it can make a physical body to use here for an hour, a day, a year, or as long as it pleases, and having for the time done with it, let that body return to its original elements.

It is then, when you, through your power, command the physical or material form of element, and can gather and compose it at will into any form you please, and also when no form of material has any power over you, that you really commence to live. The Christ of Judea had grown to this power. Though his physical body was destroyed for his use on the cross, he was able to materialize another body, with which he appeared to certain of his friends.

Thought is an Element.

The "spiritual memory" is what you bring into the world, or rather what your spirit brings to the earth stratum of life with each new incarnation. It brings the substance or wisdom gathered from its last physical life, as well as all other previous lives, but not the recollection of the events, details, and experiences by which such wisdom was gathered. Your spirit did retain the recollection of its last physical life up or near to the period of your present reincarnation. But, with a new body, there came also its new physical organ or photographic plate of memory for taking physical impressions, and on this could only be imprinted the scenes, events, and surroundings of this, your present physical existence.

Your memory of each of your physical lives is only temporarily obscured, not blotted out. As your real, your spiritual self, grows in power, as your more powerful spiritual senses develop, of which your physical senses are a coarse and very inferior counterpart, so will your spiritual memory increase in power; and this memory can, at some period of your real existence, bring to you, as you desire, recollections of the physical life of all your past existences.

What your spiritual memory now brings you is vague and incomplete as compared to what it will bring in a greater condition of ripeness. Yet many an intention, many an idea that now you may think as whimsical and visionary, comes of the force and prompting of the spiritual memory.

But you will find in time that you will not care or need as an addition to your happiness to recall near

Thought is an Element.

as much of your past, especially its darker experiences, as now you think you would, had you the power. Because your life will be an *eternal now* of happiness, and ever-increasing happiness, as your powers increase, as you learn more and more how to live, as you realize more and more the endless variety of life's pleasures, as not only you see but feel a pleasure, beauty, sublimity, grandeur, in every form of nature.

Every physical thing, every house, tree, or rock, every meeting of people in halls or churches, in families or restaurants, in the march or conflict of armies; every event, small or great in your life, has its counterpart, or, as it may be termed, reflection in element unseen to the physical eye. Every event in all your past lives is actually a part of you in unseen element. In your spirit is wrapped the power of calling back in a series of pictures, as one event is linked to another, all these parts of yourself, extending to a most remote past. Byron, in speaking of the soul's future, suggests this possibility in these words:—

>"Before creation-peopled earth,
>   Its eyes shall roll through chaos back
>To where the furthest heaven had birth;
>   The spirit trace its rising track.
>And where the future mars or makes
>   Its glance dilate o'er all shall be,
>While sun is quenched or system breaks,
>   Fixed in its own eternity."

Like the physical eye, so in the present **spiritual** conditions, the physical organ of memory is **subject**

Thought is an Element.

to decay. But every picture it takes is transferred to the eternal and indestructible organ of the spiritual. The physical memory is but the "blotter," or temporary book, for setting down the items; the book thrown aside when full, but not before every item is written in the ledger. This, the ledger of the spiritual self, is the book, and the only book, which, in the Revelations of the New Testament it is said, shall be opened, when you stand face to face with all the acts of your own life, and are judged by the god in yourself.

The imprint of the events happening through countless ages of your many physical existences, so transferred from the physical to the spiritual memory, begets the spiritual memory of experience, and out of experience is born wisdom. An old spirit, a spirit of many experiences and lives, *feels* quicker, through its inward teaching, or intuition, what is true, and what is false, than cruder and younger spirits. You *feel* a certain statement, an assertion, which may seem visionary, or ridiculous, to those around you, to be true, or have some truth in it. That comes of the action of what, for want of clearer words, we must call the spiritual memory. You cannot give for this any clear "reason" to many other minds. Has not time often proved that your *feeling*, in this respect, was correct, though through the influence, pressure, and working of the more material mind about you, may, at times, have doubted the truth of this feeling?

You are not an individual, a man, a woman, in the

Thought is an Element.

ordinary sense. You are a ceaseless current of event, surrounding experience; a series of pictures of all you have done, or have been extending, far, far back into the dim, the awful past of eternity, which no eye has pierced, or can ever pierce; and this current, commencing in an atom, a speck of being of life, has gone on accumulating more and more experience, growing in thought broader and deeper; a power moving and operating in space, gathering fresh force and insight with each new experience, until you are what now you are. And so, ever gathering force (you are to), you must grow on and on, a wonder, even to yourself, as you begin to realize that you are, indeed, "fearfully and wonderfully made." And more: the more you grow, the more are you to see, and the clearer must you see your past,—a past extending to periods beyond this earth's organization into its present condition; a past full of mysteries, even to the clearest sight of the higher world of spirit. For, since there could in spaceless universe have been no beginning, so you, in the fullest sense, can have had no beginning.

Thought is an Element.

SELF-TEACHING:

OR,

THE ART OF LEARNING HOW TO LEARN.

COPYRIGHTED, 1888, BY F. J. NEEDHAM.

It is a commonly received opinion, that in youth it is easier to learn than in after years; that at "middle age," or after, the mind becomes, as it were, set in a rut or mould, which does not readily receive new impressions. This idea is expressed in the adage: "You can't teach an old dog new tricks."

People have made this a truth by accepting it as a truth. It is not a truth. If your mind is allowed to grow and strengthen, it will learn easier and quicker than during the infancy of the body. It will learn more and more quickly *how* to learn any new thing. Learning *how* to learn, learning how to grasp at the principles underlying any art, is a study and a science by itself.

The child, in most cases, does not learn so quickly as many suppose. Think of the years often spent at school, from the age of six up to sixteen or eighteen, and how little, relatively, is learned during that period. But this time of life is not regarded as of so much importance as that after eighteen or twenty. He or she would be deemed as having a **dull intel-**

lect, who should require fourteen years to gain what a large proportion of children do gain from the age of six to twenty.

It is possible for any man or woman whose mind has grown to that degree, that they can acknowledge that every possibility exists within themselves to learn any art, any profession, any business, and become skilled therein, and this even without teachers, and at the period termed "middle age," or after; providing,

First, That they are in living earnest to learn.

Second, That they fight obstinately against the idea of "can't," or that they are too old to learn.

Third, That in all effort to become proficient in their new calling, they cease such effort so soon as it becomes fatiguing or irksome, and that they make of such effort a recreation, and not a drudgery.

Fourth, That they allow no other person to argue, sneer, or ridicule them out of the truth that the human mind can accomplish anything it sets its forces persistently upon.

Fifth, That they keep their minds in the attitude of ever desiring, demanding, praying for whatever quality or trait of character or temperament they need to succeed in their effort; and that whenever the thought of such effort is in mind, it shall be accompanied with this unspoken thought: "I will do what I have set out to do."

There should be no "hard study," at any age. Real "study" is easy and pleasing mental effort; as when you watch the motion of an animal that awakens your curiosity, of a person that interests you. You are studying when you admire and examine the structure of a beautiful flower; you are studying the method and style of an actor or actress when they most hold and compel your attention and admiration. All admiration is in reality study. When you admire anything that is beautiful, your mind is concentrated upon it. You are quite unconsciously examining it. You remember, without effort, many of its features, or characteristics. That unforced examination and attention is study.

To "study hard" is to try to admire; to try to admire is to try to love; to try to love, or to be forced by others to try to love, generally ends in hating the thing or pursuit so forced upon you, — one reason why so often the schoolboy hates "to learn his lesson."

The experience of those who have gone before us in any art, trade, occupation, or profession, is unquestionably valuable, but valuable *only* as suggestion. There is a great deal laid down as rules and "canons of art" which shackle and repress originality. The idea is constantly, though indirectly, impressed on learners, that the utmost limit of perfection has been reached in some art by some "old master," and that it would be ridiculous to think of surpassing him.

Now, genius knows no "old master." It knows no set form of rules made for it by others. It makes its own rules as it goes along, as did Shakespeare, Byron, and Scott, in literature, and the first Napoleon in war; and your mind may have in it **the seed**

Thoughts are Things.

of some new idea, discovery, invention, some new rendering of art in some form, which the world never saw before.

Any man or woman who loves to look at trees and flowers, lakes and rivulets, waves, waterfalls, and clouds, has within them the faculty for imitating them in the effects of light, shade, and color, — has, in brief, a taste for painting.

You say, "People to be artists, must have the art born within them." I say, "If they admire the art, they have within them the faculty for advance in that art."

You say, "But because I admire a rose, or a landscape, is no sign I can ever paint either." I say, "Yes, you can, providing you really want to."

But how? Put your effort on it for an hour, half an hour, fifteen minutes, a day. Commence. Commence anywhere. Anything in this world will do for a starting-point. Commence, and try to imitate on paper a dead leaf, a live one, a stone, a rock, a log, a box, a brickbat. A brickbat lying in the mud has lying with it light, shade, and color, and the laws governing them, as much as a cathedral, and is a better foundation than a cathedral to commence on. Commence with the stub of a pencil, on the back of an old envelope. Every minute of such work after commencement is so much practice gained. Every minute before such commencement, providing you intend to commence, and do not, is so much practice lost, as regards that particular art.

Mind, though, you make of such practice a recreation, just as boys do in ball throwing and catching, or as the billiard player does who takes up the cue for half an hour, matched only against himself, or as the horseman does who exercises the horse for practice before the race. When the work becomes irksome, when you get out of patience, because your brickbat won't come out on the paper like the original, drop it, wait for your patience-reservoir to fill up, and take for your next copy a log, a tree trunk, or anything else.

You say that you should go to a teacher of this or that art, so that you can become "properly grounded in its principles," and that, by such teacher's aid, you shall avoid blundering and stumbling along, making little or no progress.

Take up any trade, any handicraft, any art, all by yourself, and grope along in it by yourself for a few weeks, and at the end of that time you will have many well-defined and intelligent questions to ask about it, of some one more experienced in it than yourself, — the teacher. That is the time to go to the teacher. The teacher should come in when an interest in the art or study is awakened. To have him before, is like answering questions before they are asked.

You cannot teach a dog to paint. The intelligence using the dog's organization has not grown to an appreciation of such imitation of natural objects. But you can teach him to draw a cart, to "point" to game in the cover, to swim out to the water-fowl you have shot, and bring it to you. Why? **Because**

Thoughts are Things.

the dog has these instincts, or desires, born in him. The trainer, his teacher, brings them out. Some men and women have no more admiration for a beautiful landscape than the dog. Of course, neither can ever be taught to paint, because they have not the desire to paint, nor the admiration of the thing to be painted.

"Then, whatever a man or woman really desires to do, is to be taken as some proof that they can do?" you ask. "Yes; that is the exact idea." *Desire to accomplish is a proof of ability to accomplish.* Of course, such ability may be weighted down and kept back by many causes, such as ill health of body, ill health of mind, unfavorable surroundings, and, perhaps, *greatest of all*, utter ignorance that such desire *is* a proof of the possession of power to accomplish the thing desired.

How did you learn to walk, and how did you learn to talk? Could any one have taught you, if desire to walk and talk had not been born with you? Did you go to a walking teacher, or a talking teacher? Did you not learn both accomplishments after ten thousand failures? So far as you can remember, was it not rather an amusement than otherwise, to learn both, or at least, was there any idea of work associated with these early efforts?

You place a boy or a girl by the water-side, and give them full liberty, and they will learn to swim as naturally as they learn to walk, because the desire to swim is in them. If, after learning, they see a better swimmer, they will naturally try to imitate him; and all this endeavor, from first to last, will be for them far more recreation than work. The better swimmer who comes along represents the teacher; and the boy or girl who can already swim fairly well, and are anxious to swim better, represent pupils who are in a fit condition to be taught.

Think for a moment, how much it was necessary to teach your body, in training it to walk. First, to balance yourself upright on two feet without falling. Secondly, to balance yourself on one foot without falling. Thirdly, to move the body. Fourthly, to give it the direction in which you wanted to go. And yet we call walking a "mechanical," and not a mental, effort.

If you are determined to paint, and love the creations of nature and art well enough to try and imitate them, you will be constantly studying effects in light and shade on rocks, stones, cliffs, towers, steeples. You will observe and study, and be rejoiced at the many changing aspects and colors of the sky, as you never were before. You will discover, as you continue to observe, that nature has a different shade of color for every day in the year, and almost every hour of the day. You will suddenly find in all this a new and permanent recreation, without money and without price. You will then find new interests and new sources of amusement in studying the works of painters and their methods, which will be revealed to you just so fast as your appreciation *grows* up to them.

The same principle will apply to any branch of mechanics or art, — to anything. Of course, it is best to pursue that for which you have the most inclination, that is, admiration for. If you are in any occupation that does not suit you, and you want to engage on some art that does suit you, if you have fifteen minutes in the day to spare, commence on that art.

If it is painting, paint a brickbat in some idle moment as well as you can, and only as a means of amusement. If it is carving, you have always the means for practice, if you have a jack-knife and a bit of wood. If it be music, a banjo or guitar with but a single string will give you means for practice. For you must commence in the simplest way, even as you crept before you walked. There *must* be imperfect effort before there can be relatively perfect result.

Because, when you do so commence, you commence to practice with one instrument far more ingenious and complicated than any you can buy for use in your art; namely, your mind.

If we commence in this way, we commence something else; we commence drawing toward us ways, means, helps, and agencies unseen, but powerful, to help us. We are not to expect success in an hour, a day, a month, a year. But if we persist, a relative success is coming all the while. The effort of this month is better than that of last. There may come periods of weariness and discouragement: periods when, as we look back, we seem to have made no advance; periods, in fact, when we seem to have gone back, when we seem doing worse than at the start; periods when we lose all interest in the work. It makes us sick to look at it, even to think of taking it up again; and a certain sense of guilt at our neglect intensifies the sickness.

That is a mistake. If, in our music, our painting, our profession, our business, be it what it may, we strive for some certain result, and fail time after time, and week after week, to effect it, yet we are still advancing toward it.

We may not see such advance. That is because the advance is not in the direction we think it should be. There may be a screw loose in a part of our mental being that we have taken no note of, which keeps us back. That screw, in very many cases, lies in the state of mind in which we take up our work or pursuit.

We may be too anxious or impatient. We take up the pen, the brush, or the tool, in a hurried frame of mind. We want to do too many things at once. Or we endeavor to crowd the doing of several things in too short a limit of time. Or we are unable to dismiss all thought, save what bears on the effort now in hand.

All such moods are destructive to the best effort. They take much of our force from that effort. A common result is that we can do nothing to suit us. We throw down our work in disgust. We may not take it up again for weeks. We do take it up at last, perhaps, in a listless, indifferent frame of mind. We do not then set our hearts on doing anything perfect, or making it come up to our ideal in a moment, *and that* IS *the very time* when we produce some new effect; when we hit the idea we have aimed **at; when** we are surprised at the apparently accidental development of a new power within us.

There is a great mystery in this, — a mystery we may never solve, — the mystery that whatever purpose this power within us we call mind sets itself upon, fixes itself upon persistently, that purpose it is accomplishing, that purpose it is carrying out, that purpose it is ever drawing nearer to itself, not only when we work for it with the body and the intellect, but we are *growing ever toward it when it seems for the time* forgotten, or when we are asleep.

That persistent purpose, that strong desire, that never-ceasing longing, is a seed in the mind. It is rooted there. It is alive. It never stops growing. Why this is so, we may never know. Perhaps it is not desirable to know. It is enough to know that it is so. There is a wonderful law involved in it. This law, when known, followed out, and trusted, leads every individual to mighty and beautiful results. This law, followed with our eyes open, leads to more and more happiness in life; but followed blindly, involuntarily with our eyes shut, leads to misery.

To succeed in any undertaking, any art, any trade, any profession, simply keep it ever persistently fixed in mind as an aim, and then study to make all effort toward it play, recreation. The moment it becomes "hard work," we are *not* advancing. I mean by "play," that both body and mind work easily and pleasantly. It matters not what a man or woman is doing, whether digging sand or scrubbing floors, when the mind is interested in that work and the muscles are full of strength, such work *is* play, and is more apt to be well done. When the muscles are exhausted of their power, and will alone drives the body forward, the occupation soon becomes work, drudgery, and is much the more apt to be ill done. I commence low down with illustration, down to sand, mud, brickbats; but the principle is the same, be the worker a hod-carrier or a Michael Angelo.

The science of learning to learn, then, involves largely that of making recreation of all effort. This is not as easy as it may seem. It involves a continual prayer for patience, patience, patience.

"Patience to play?" you ask. Yes. When we are amused by any effort of our own, be it effort of the eye, in seeing sights that please it, or effort of the ear, in hearing sounds that please it, or effort of muscle, in exercising them, that is the very time when we are most attentive and most absorbed. The very time when we forget there is such a thing as patience, is the very time we most exercise patience.

That is the mood we need to cultivate. Because moods of mind determine the character and quality of effort. The painter writes out his mood in his picture; a mistake, a blur, a defect, a daub, may write out in that picture too much hurry to get ahead. He took up his brush, possibly, full of irritation, because his wife asked him for more money for household expenses; result, he puts a woman in that picture twelve feet high as proportioned to other objects, when she should have been but four. What put on that extra and needless eight feet? **A mood** born of household expenses. Or the scrubber wrote out her mood of mind on the floor. Where? In that neglected corner, where the last dust of summer lingers alone. Why? Because her mood of hurry to be through with her work is there written; or her mood of dishonesty, in doing as little as possible for the money to be received; or her mood of anxiety concerning the sick child, left at home in some squalid tenement; or the poor woman's mood born of physical weakness, in thus trying to do a man's work, with no nutritious food in her stomach, and no money to buy any till the work is done.

My very practical friend, you who despise all "art flummery," all and everything that is not "business," and smells of wood, or stone, or leather, or bank-bills, this cultivation of the mood is of vast importance to you, also; because, when you meet your brother Hard Cash, to have a wrangle over bargain and sale, the man who is in the coolest mood, the most collected mood, the mood most free of other thought, or care, the man who is in the least hurry, the man who throws overboard all anxiety as to results, the man who is not too eager, who can lay back in his chair and make a joke or laugh at one, when millions are trembling in the balance, who keeps all his reserve force till it is needed, that is the man who can play the best hand in your game, and make the best bargain. That is the man who gains his end by some knowledge of spiritual law; and spiritual law can be used for all purposes, and purposes relatively low as well as high; and in some things the wicked, so-

Thoughts are Things.

called, of today, are better informed in some phases of spiritual law than those who call themselves good.

How shall we get ourselves, then, into the most desirable mood for doing our best? By praying for it, asking for it, demanding it, in season and out of season. We can wish an earnest desire in a second, no matter where we are. That is a prayer. It is a thought that goes out, and does its work in bringing us another atom of the quality desired. That atom is never lost. It adds itself to and adds its strength to all the other atoms of the same quality so gained. So you call this simple? Is the method too easy? Remember, we are indeed fearfully and wonderfully made; and when Solomon wrote this he had an inkling of the existence of powers wrapped up in human bodies, that startled him, and would us, did we more fully realize them.

Possibly this question may be asked: "What is the use of cultivating, or encouraging others to cultivate any form of art, when for thousands the struggle is so hard today for bread?" Or, in other words, "What is the use of educating people to wants and desires they cannot satisfy?" Or, "What bearing and benefit has art cultivation in righting the 'great wrongs' of the hour?"

It is of the greatest possible benefit. Art, art appreciation, art cultivation, refines human nature. Refinement demands finer surroundings, finer food, finer houses, cleaner houses, cleaner clothes, cleaner skins. You can't make people clean, neat, tasteful, by telling them they "ought" to be so. They must

Thoughts are Things.

have brought out of them some calling, some occupation, some work which will implant ever-increasing desire for more of the elegancies of life. Much of what is called the "oppression" of the strong over the weak, the rich over the poor, comes because so many of the poor do not aspire above a pig-pen under the window, a mud-puddle in the back yard, and a front garden growing tomato cans, dead cats, and old hoop-skirts. Much of the money today given in charity to the poor, is really poured from one rich man's pocket into that of another, and relieves only a temporary distress. You roll a half a ton of coal this winter into the poor man's cellar. His family are warmed for the hour. The profits go into the safe of the coal corporation. Its heat warms human beings with little ambition above animals. You encourage that man's boy or girl to paint ever so roughly with the cheapest of water colors, to mould forms in clay, to have any faculty awakened which shall show them what a beautiful world they really live in, and soon with this there may come a growing distaste for the mud-puddle in the back yard, and the display of hoop-skirts and tomato cans in the front. You show those children that they have within them more or less of this mighty and mysterious element — mind, and that through its exercise they can become almost anything to which they aspire, and that the more of the Infinite Spirit they call to themselves, the more will they have to strengthen, beautify, enrich, invigorate, and electrify their souls and bodies, and you have then started them on the road of doing for themselves, by the powers in themselves. They are then on a road leading away from both charitable soup-kitchens and gin-shops. If they cultivate the love for grace and beauty in any direction, they cultivate also an ability for expressing such grace and beauty. If they follow the law of persistent demand for improvement in such grace or beauty, whether it be by the exercise of pen or tongue, of painting or sculpture, or self-command, or polish of manner, or the art of actor, elocutionist, musician, or worker on stone, worker in metal, cultivator of plant, tree, flower, they will at last do something a *little better* than anyone else can do in their peculiar way, and through their self-taught, peculiar method; and when they can do this, the world will gladly come to them, and bring them its dollars and cents, for what they can please it with.

None of us know what is in us till we try to bring it out. A man, a woman, may go their whole life with some wonderful power, some remarkable talent which would benefit and please mankind, feeling it ever from time to time, struggling for expression in a desire to use it, in a longing to express it, yet having it ever forced back by that fatal thought, "I can't." "It's no use." "It's ridiculous, the idea of my aspiring to such a thing." We are treasure boxes, holding wondrous powers. We brought these treasures with us into the world from an immeasurably far-off past — a past we may not compute — a past of the spirit, born into being, the tiniest **atom**,

---

Thoughts are Things.

the faintest movement, drawing to itself ever, age after age, through unconscious exercise of desire or demand, more and more of power, more and more of complex organization, more and more of variety of talent, more and more of the marvellous power coming through combination and recombination of element, until at last the man is born, the woman is born, blind at first, blind as millions now are regarding the wealth within them; blind to faith and belief in themselves, until the veil is pulled from their eyes, and then they shall soon spring up into gods, destined to a career of eternal life, eternal growth, and eternal and illimitable happiness.

Thoughts are Things.

HOW TO PUSH YOUR BUSINESS.

Copyrighted, 1888, by F. J. Needham.

No matter what position you are in, be it clerk, typewriter, porter, bookkeeper, car conductor, an employee in a factory or elsewhere, if you make up your mind or fall into the way of thinking that you are always to remain where you are, and never rise any higher, or receive more for your services, the chances are very largely against your rising. You make those chances against you by keeping in that state of mind in which you see yourself in the future as occupying that same position. You make chances in your favor by seeing yourself in what you call imagination on the rise.

The state of mind you are most in is a force pushing for or against your business and welfare. One permanent state of mind will bring to you success and another failure.

There are those born with minds so lacking in aim, purpose, and method, that they cannot provide for themselves at all. They cannot even keep what is left them by their parents. These are examples of permanent states of mind which bring failure.

There are those born in material poverty, who pile up great wealth almost from the start. These are instances of another permanent state of mind

Thoughts are Things.

which, putting its thought always on a purpose, brings success, so far as the mere making of money is success.

The pushing of any kind of business always commences first in the mind. The man who is today controlling a dozen railroads, commenced in some relatively humble position. But in mind he was always aiming higher. When he gained a step ahead, he did not in mind stop there, in imagination he was on the next step.

But the man for years a rag-picker and scavenger, has never looked or aimed any higher. He sees himself always a rag-picker. In his thoughts he never gets beyond the rag-picker's limits. He may envy people who are better off. He may wish for some of the things they enjoy. But he never says in thought, "I am going to get out of this occupation. I am going into something higher, cleaner, and more remunerative." So he remains always a rag-picker.

If you keep always in a low, unaspiring state of mind, if you look on the best and most beautiful things in this world as things you never can have or enjoy, if you see yourself always at the foot of the ladder, grumbling at those above you, then at the foot of the ladder you are very likely to stay.

Any state of mind you are in for any length of time will carry you to things in the material world in conformity to that state. If you are very fond of horses, and think of them a great deal, you are very likely to go, when opportunity offers, where you can see the finest horses, and where others fond of horses go. You are then the more likely to be led to talk to some one about horses. You are also the more likely to become engaged in something connected with the buying, or keeping, or caring for horses. But it was the thought that led you first into the kingdom of horse-flesh.

If your fondness for horses goes no farther than the desire to be among them, and you are always saying in thought, "I can only be a hostler or a driver," and you hold yourself aloof (in mind) from the wealthy owners of stock, then always a hostler you will be. But if you say, "I am going to get up in this business, I have as good a right to own a stable as any one else," you are then very likely to own a stable.

Why? Because that very state of mind brings you nearer the men who do own stables. They feel your thought unconsciously, and when you are alert and civil, and as much interested in their business as if it were you own (as you must be when you are in the pushing, aspiring state of mind), they begin to feel an interest in you. You will have more and more opportunities to talk with them. They find you useful. They find, probably, at last, that they cannot get on without you. Out of this comes friendship. Friendship sets you up in business, or assists you in some way. There is a great deal of "friendship in trade." Men are dependent on each other for assistance in every branch of business.

If, when among people, you carry always with **you** the thought of self-depreciation, and think of yourself as of little value or use, those about you **will not** treat you with that deference or respect **as if you**

Thoughts are Things.

regarded yourself more highly; nor will they feel disposed to help you to any higher position. Now, are you fit for any higher position, so long as you lower yourself in your own mind?

You may find, on searching into yourself, that there are positions in life now apparently beyond your reach, in which you *dare* not see yourself. Probably nine hotel scrubbing women out of ten would not dare or entertain seriously for a moment the thought that they might some day control the hotel of which they are the humblest part. But occasionally a person does rise from some similar position to one far higher. That person dared to think of him or herself in such higher position. This was the unseen moving force that carried him there.

Wherever you put yourself in mind, and persistently keep yourself, towards such position you will be carried. You may not gain the actual place aimed at, but you will stand somewhere near it, which is better than standing in the gutter of aimlessness and hopelessness.

Dare, then, and live, now in mind as the head of a business, or the head of a department for whose workings you are entirely responsible. You are then attracting to you the unseen forces which will put you in such places. But if you will not aspire above the place of a wage-worker, you put out the force which will always keep you a mere worker for weekly wages. If you are afraid of taking responsibilities, and desire only what you think the safe corner of sure and steady wages, you will always remain in that corner, more or less a machine moved at the pleasure of others, and obliged, possibly, to see the larger profits of your skill going to others.

It is he or she who dares to take responsibilities that best succeeds. If you dare not, you *must* remain the poorer paid help of those who dare.

Dare to think of yourself now as a leader in business, and as a handler of great sums of money. So to dare in your own secret mind exposes you to no ridicule from others. It is as cheap so to see yourself as to imagine yourself always at the foot of the ladder. Cultivate the art of expecting success. Confident expectation of success is the most useful habit of mind or method of using your thought-force you can cultivate. Constant expectation of misfortune, disaster, and bad luck is the most ruinous method of using your thought-force, and is a sure road to poverty.

Responsibilities need not bring anxiety, fret, and worry. Spiritual or mental power dismisses the thought of responsibilities, until it is proper and profitable to think of them. The lack of it causes the proprietor of a small grocery to lie awake half the night, worrying over his affairs, and getting up in the morning less fitted for business than ever, while the millionaire dealer in the same articles throws care off his mind, and is able to sleep and gather strength for the morrow's effort.

There is as much actual money in a nation (other than of gold, silver, or legalized bank notes) as there is of paper passing from hand to hand used as **money**, and accepted as money, bearing the names of **private** individuals, or issued in the shape of **bonds or stocks**

Thoughts are Things.

by companies of individuals. You would readily accept the note of a Gould or Vanderbilt, promising to pay you a certain sum at a certain time, and this piece of paper you can today use as money. So the Gould or Vanderbilt can issue a money of his own. So, to an extent, can any merchant or financier of undoubted credit. Then there is as much money in the nation (other than in coin or legalized bank bills) as there are bits of paper bearing the names of men of sound credit, or of companies or corporations, which pledge themselves to pay certain sums at a certain time. If you believe these individuals or corporations to have a great deal of money, you will readily take their promise to pay, on a bit of paper, as money. There is then no limit to the amount of money which can be and is put out in this way. There is not of gold or silver, coin or regular bank bills, near enough in any of our great cities to carry on all its daily business. The rest is made of men's names, commanding credit at the bottom of notes, promising to pay at certain dates, or of pieces of paper known as stocks or bonds, which, if in your hands, represents a piece of a railroad, or a line of steamers, or other property.

As the maker of some article of value and use, as the projector of some enterprise which will give people comfort and amusement, you can gain the confidence of others, and with such confidence credit. Your name also on a piece of paper can pass from hand to hand, and have the value of money. The more confidence people have in your honesty and ability, the firmer based is its value. Despite all appearances to the contrary, all business is today based on faith in the honesty and intention, either of men, or corporations, or governments, to act up to their promises.

The world needs better things than it ever had before,—better houses, better foods, better amusements, new recreations, new devices in art. It is constantly wanting, and paying well for the best. Do not in your mind say you cannot devise and push something better before it. You can. To say in your heart you can't, is to put an impassable barrier between you and your possibilities.

To say you can't, is to commit one of the violations of the law for using and enjoying the best goods of this world. To say, "I can," and "I will," is to put yourself within reach of the thought-current which will bring wealth to you.

If you are satisfied that the article you offer people, be it your invention, your ideas, your writings, has a certain value, and you do not demand that value, you do an injustice to yourself; and an injustice done to self is an injustice and injury done to many others. For, if by so doing you starve or become sick, you become a care and encumbrance on others. If in your mind you put out continually the thought that your article is justly worth what you ask for it, other minds will *feel* that thought or force, and rate it and value it as you do. If yours is a good article, and in mind you depreciate it, **you** send from you the force which makes others **depreciate it, and you with it. If you took a tray of genuine diamonds to sell on the street, and you felt,** looked, and acted as if you were doubtful of their being diamonds, ninety-nine out of one hundred who looked at them would, through your own mental action on their minds, take those diamonds for glass or paste; and the chances are very strong that the man who did recognize them as diamonds, would try to cheat you, by confirming your doubt and delusion as to their real value. This, your unjust depreciation of yourself and your work, is another violation of the law for gaining the best the world has for you.

If you are continually improving the article you make, and keep it properly before the world, the world will find out that improvement, and seek it and pay for it. If you make the cheap article, the sham, the counterfeit or imitation, the buying world, which is willing to pay a high price, but insists, and justly, on getting the worth of its money, will at last avoid you. Where does all the cheap trash go? Into the cheapest stores, to be sold at the smallest profit. As you cut down wages to make the article cheaper, you are certain to get the poorer work for such wages. Your work is then done in a hurry. No heart, no love, no interest is put in it. It is the competition for cheapness, the rivalry to undersell others, the desire to pander to buyers who want everything cheap, that makes cheap clothing, which is rotten before being put on; cheap houses, which sometimes tumble to pieces before being finished; cheap food, which is half rottenness; cheap plumbing, which fills houses with foul air, and causes expensive funerals. Could this delusion of cheapness have full sway, and prevail over nature's laws, this very planet would be made over at a "great reduction in price," and we should be furnished with second-rate air and sunshine. Fortunately, the wonderful workings of the eternal power for good is ever toward constant improvement and refinement, as it has manifested itself in the growth of this earth from the chaos, crudity, and imperfection existing countless ages ago, to its present improved condition; and this condition must ripen into one of far greater improvement, as more light and knowledge of more law dawns upon it, and men and women see, as they will, that eternal happiness and eternal prosperity are based on eternal right and eternal justice.

The more you spend wisely in any business, the more will you make. The more you expend in making your place of business attractive and tasteful, the more of the better class of customers does it, by a sure-working law, attract to you. Ornament your business in mind, first, and keep to the determination so to ornament it. You have then set in operation the magnet, the thought-power which will draw the means to pay for such ornamentation. This law is followed in successful business all about us. The fashionable tailor locates his shop on the fashionable thoroughfare, pays a high rent, imports the most costly cloths, and employs the best skill in his work. By these means he attracts the best paying customers. He charges, and justly, a high price. His profits are proportionately large. That man previously created his business in his mind. He did it, possibly, when a workman on the board of a cheap shop in a squalid street. The force he so **generated** in that shop, carried him out of it to the better one. His brother workmen, having no such imaginings, envied others richer than they, and so expended force in envy, which lowers, instead of aspiration, which inevitably carries upward, and, as a result, drudge in the cheap shop still. Your thoughts carry you up or down, according as you use them. You *must* make the thing — the place in life you fill — in your mind years before you fill it.

You are now, in your thought, making some future place for yourself, pleasant or unpleasant.

Keep away from despondent, discouraged people, who are always expecting and thereby courting ill luck. If much in their association, be they whom they may, you will surely absorb of their thought, think it, and unconsciously act it. You will not see successful methods clearly. Your brain will be muddled. You are half them and but half yourself. You are then attracting of their ruinous thought-element, and in its current.

Men of success gravitate naturally towards other men of success. It is not a "mere superstition" which prompts some to avoid unlucky men. Our powerful corporations are made up of men of like order of spiritual force, confident, bold, hopeful, pushing, determined. They follow this part of the law. Their success is for the most part a one-sided one, for they do not follow the whole law.

I mean by a "one-sided success" that success which gains wealth at the expense of health, and in its absorption for money getting only, loses nearly all capacity to enjoy what money can bring.

Thoughts are Things.

Absorption of the inferior, despondent thought of another, has ruined many an enterprise. You may see today a clear plan of action. You feel hopeful and confident. Tomorrow all is reversed. You have lost faith in your idea. You see only failure. You are down cellar. Why? Because, in all probability, you have been mingling with aimless, discouraged people. Even though you did not talk to them of your project, their inferior thought has flown to you. It sticks to you like pitch. It has colored, clouded, and befogged all your views. Your mind today is half that of one or more person's who lives steeped in a thought-atmosphere of dependence, discouragement, and gloom. It is as true that the thought of others can enter into our being, and become for a time a part of it, as that dampness or foul air can permeate your house or your clothing. It is thus that "evil communications corrupt good manners." It is difficult to touch the pitch of inferior thought without being defiled.

Why does the chief of American financiers seclude himself so much from people? Because, consciously or unconsciously, he lives up to that law, of which he realizes enough to know that to keep his head clear, he must avoid the confused thought-atmosphere of the great mass of people. Napoleon got his plans in the seclusion of the closet and the country. In all the varied and wonderful workings of the element of mind upon mind, this law stands of the first importance.

Worse still, through this absorption of inferior thought, you may be enslaved and ruled by inferior

Thoughts are Things.

minds. Today many a brilliant and powerful mind is so ruled. They feel they know more than those about them, and still follow unwillingly the methods prescribed by the inferior. As a result, they are slaves where they should be masters. In this way is confidence and courage crushed almost out, and by the same crushing of their spirits is physical health lost, also.

Thousands of beggars are made through the brutal dominion of the strong will over minds so enslaved, not always because theirs are the weakest, but because, unconsciously or timorously, they allow such ascendency.

Say to yourself continually, "I will not allow myself so to be enslaved by any one," and you are putting out the force which will cut you a path out of slavery, dependence, and beggary.

When you are confident, determined, pushing, hopeful, and buoyant, and, above all, your business is based on RIGHT and JUSTICE, the world will *feel* you as a rising man. It will feel you before it knows you personally. It is the unseen world of thought which so feels you. Your thought is then in the current of success, the current which constructs, builds up, and accomplishes results. It is a literal unseen force or element acting for success, and acting on and with other minds putting out the same force and with similar motives. Then as more and more you put forward your business, you in turn, your enterprise, the minds who can aid you, and by your effort be aided, are prepared to have confidence in you. Confidence is the basis of credit,

Thoughts are Things.

and the power which puts loans and bank-notes in your hands, to use for bringing to you more. To *use*, and ever *use*, mind you, in projecting new enterprises; to spend, also, for yourself, for all that makes life bright and happy; to circulate, but *not to hoard*.

If you overtask body and brain to gain money (as so many do), it does you no good. You have not lived up to the highest applications of the law. The mortality among the leading retail dry-goods merchants of New York City for the last ten years has been remarkable. The strain caused by the competition of cheapness, and the necessity which binds them year in and year out to one business, with so little of variation or recreation, has cut them off, even in their prime. To gain money at the expense of health, is to cut off your feet and sell them for a pair of boots.

Business can be pushed successfully without fagging or making yourself its slave. If you are fagged, it is evidence of an unsound part in your business. When mind and body work harmoniously together, the greatest force is developed. That force, properly placed two hours a day in a business, will accomplish more than ten hours of "puttering" and "pottering" about.

You cannot push a business you do not love. You cannot push a business in which you put no heart. You cannot push or succeed in any business unless you take a continual interest and pleasure in improving it, expanding it. Love for a business brings continually new thoughts, plans, ideas, and devices for

Thoughts are Things.

so improving it. Love for a business brings new force ever to push that business.

You cannot succeed in a business unless in mind you are ever increasing and expanding that business. All great enterprises are thought over and lived over and over again in thought by their projectors, long before the material results are seen. The thought or plan in advance is the real construction of unseen element. When firmly held to, it is adding ever to itself of more force, idea, device; and when so held to, draws to itself material things and results, by the same law by which the lump of metal in solution draws to itself crystallization of the same metal out of that solution.

The man or woman who succeeds in any business is always in mind living ahead of their business of today. What is being accomplished today was planned, thought over, and lived in, months, possibly years, before. That plan, steadfastly adhered to, was the force that carried the business ahead. It was the power that pushed it.

If you are in a small business, and always in mind see yourself in that small business, you will always remain in a small business. Live in mind in the larger store, workshop, or office, the better cultivated farm, and you will find the better and larger, be it what it may, gradually moving in upon you. If you keep a peanut stand, see yourself, in imagination, the proprietor of a fruit store, and into the fruit store you will go.

When you cease planning expansion and improvement in a business, that business begins to die. It

Thoughts are Things.

will for a time seem to flourish, but the newer enterprise in the same direction, born of some other energetic brain, is growing and going ahead of it. Fifty years ago there were prosperous dry-goods merchants in New York City, who imagined that their business would be done by the same methods in which they had all their lives been accustomed to do it. A. T. Stewart came, developed a new method, and the old firms went out of sight. Stewart applied but a part of the law. Therefore his was but a partial success. He gained money, it is true; but the mere gain of money is not the perfected success of the business of the future.

Important business plans should be often talked over, but should be talked *only* with those whose interests and motives are like your own. They should be so talked or discussed at a regular time, and always, if possible, in one place or room. If you talk them out in promiscuous places, in the street, the restaurant, the railway station, you will lose power, and give away your secrets, even though no physical ears hear you. The quotation that "walls have ears," involves a truth. Agencies unseen, busy, prying, meddlesome, are always near in public places or any other room than your own, and will snatch from you your secrets, and impress them in the minds of others.

When you have a room devoted to the peaceful discussion of your plans, and this room is long used, you make in that room a thought-atmosphere, or a force favorable to your business. It will become stronger and stronger. You will in that **room, when** you so talk, get new ideas quicker than elsewhere. You make, then, a place, also, where new ideas and suggestions can be dropped in your mind. But if you indulge in heated or angry argument with others, or your mind in secret is angered, you create a force injurious to your welfare in any direction.

Your real wife is your best "partner" in your business. Your real wife, your complement or completement (for the divinely wedded man and woman form the complete whole) is, if not now by your side physically, in existence somewhere, either in the material or spiritual world. If she be with you here materially, she will prove herself, by taking a live interest in your business, and in all that concerns your welfare. If you heed her intuitions, her impressions for good or ill regarding individuals with whom you deal, her feelings for or against your proposed acts, her suggestions regarding future advancement, things will go well with you. If you sneer at her impressions, opinions, or suggestions, as a "woman's fancies," if you take the reins entirely in your own hands, assuming, as some men do assume, that women "know nothing about business," and that her place is entirely within the domain of the house, if in so doing you repress her speech and snub her into silence, you cripple your strongest aid, you blur and blind the feminine eye, which, if rightly used and trained, will always see in advance farther than the masculine, and in so doing give to her husband the idea, plan, or suggestion, which he alone can work out.

Thoughts are Things.

THE RELIGION OF THE DRAMA.

COPYRIGHT, 1888, BY F. J. NEEDHAM.

WHATEVER in art, in song, in poetry, in painting, in oratory or elocution, in the expression of emotion or sentiment by music or muscular movement, compels our admiration, interests us, and causes us, for the time being, to forget ourself or occupation, has the effect of resting our minds. If the mind or spirit is rested, the body is always rested. Mind and body in this way are literally re-created with new thought-element (for thought is element), and the highest, the finest, the purest expression of sentiment, being the most powerful and healthful order of thought, can be and is absorbed by us as sent from him or her who expresses it, and being so absorbed is a source of rest and strength, a vigor and a medicine, to the mind and body. The stage concentrates and masses, as to time and place, many arts and talents — poetry, painting, music, oratory (for all inspired acting is a species of oratory). It must have the best service of the writer, the dramatist, the architect and decorator in the construction and ornamentation of the theatre, the best service of the mechanic in the complicated mechanism for spectacle and scenery. It calls to its aid chemistry, in the generation of light and color for scenic effect. Directly or indirectly, there is scarcely an art or science you can name but whose help or aid the stage requires. The employment of all this art can, in an hour, rest a thousand or two thousand people, divert their thought or the attitude of their minds temporarily from their cares or occupations, and rest and recuperate those departments of mind employed on such occupations.

The artists, if inspired by love of their art, are also rested and recuperated by the exercise of such art, for all inspiration is an invigorator and re-creator. It is only when the artist tries to force or simulate inspiration that such, to him, irksome effort exhausts, as all irksome effort exhausts. The actors or singers are also re-created, re-invigorated, warmed, cheered in mind and benefited in body by the flow to them, in thought-element, of sympathy, admiration, and appreciation from their audiences.

Religion, as I understand it, means the law governing all things,—the law governing all life, the law ruling all human life to greater and greater happiness, the law of the infinite and eternal spirit of good, of which spirit we are all parts and partakers — and in the cultivation and expression of every talent, we glorify God and bring more of God and of Life to earth. The use or benefit to people in any art or talent is the religion involved in that thing.

The drama, then, when properly used, is a re-creator and an invigorator of human minds. The pulpit is very near the stage, for in it stands the man who represents, or should represent, the highest result as to power of human aspiration; the priest,—or as the word indicates, the chief prayer or chief aspirer,— whose effort it is and whose pleasure and recreation it is, not only to receive from higher sources the LAST UNFOLDMENT of truth, the last revelation of the law of life, and convey it to his hearers, but to illustrate it and make it clearer by every device of parable or comparison, to make its presentation forcible through the disciplined action on his body of the force born of zeal and enthusiasm in his spirit, which is the essence of oratory; to be DRAMATIC in speech and action, not in the general and stilted application of that word, but dramatic as throwing on his hearers a whole drama in a few sentences.

The greatest actor and artist will always be a student, an observer, an admirer, a worshipper of all things in Nature; and he or she who admires and appreciates worships, and whoever worships Nature worships the unseen and incomprehensible Force of which all things seen of the physical eye are a manifestation; and whoever so worships comes nearer and nearer to God in proportion to the depth and intensity of their appreciation of Nature in her physical or outward form. Whoever so worships becomes capable of *feeling* more and more emotion. Such FEEL more and more of the Infinite Spirit entering into them and becoming a part of them. Whoever so feels can also most express such feeling, whether by speech or gesture, or even the silent pose of body which sometimes, in moments of dramatic delineation, carries a power which thrills an audience to that silence worth more than noisy bursts of applause. It is at such moments that the living, intense, quivering soul, the thought of the **artist, is acting on the collective mind of his audience, as the** rays of light converged to a focus in the electric lamp stream out far and wide, coloring to its own shade everything on which it falls.

You cannot simulate or imitate mechanically any emotion, and have such simulation taken for an expression of infinite force working through you, by such as have God, or the highest and finest appreciation of God's power, in themselves. But you can trade upon an emotion which you may feel to an extent at one moment and throw yourself out of the next. The beggar who cries to excite your sympathy calls to his aid, and connects his spirit temporarily with, the thought current of grief or distress. He feels the action upon him of such order or element of thought. But there is always to the quickest ear, the most honest nature, the keenest sense that feels the thought of others, a base ring in such expression of grief; and the actor or artist in any department of expression, who feels an emotion or sentiment at one moment and laughs at the next, is not the most devout artist, for he or she lacks reverence for their profession, for their genius, for the power of the infinite working through them. This is the real blasphemy. This is taking and feeling God's power on the lips and in the heart at one moment, and mocking it directly afterward; and though success may for a time attend such adulterated expressions of genius, it will never bring the highest success. It will be effort bringing in seen or unseen existence its inevitable penalty, for neither art or existence ceases with the wearing out of this earthly instrument — the body. The time must come when every sinner is brought face to face with his own sin, and not only the sin but all its results in the past,—its pretences of admiration from others, its pretended friendship based only on low motive,—and so hideous may it all appear, that such sinner may call upon the mountains to fall upon and cover him.

God is law, and God cannot be mocked. The religion of the drama leads to temperance in all things.

No artist nor actor, no singer, no dancer, can afford to dissipate life's forces in any kind of intemperance. Art of any kind gives a solid reason against excess in eating or drinking, or the exhaustion that comes of anger or evil thinking, for the force so expended is just so much force taken from that art; and the actor or singer who goes upon the stage with his powers weakened by any excess, soon learns in some way that his services are not as desirable as he would have them; and although genius may shine for a time, despite the wrong it inflicts upon itself, yet, at last, genius, as we often see, goes down and out of sight when it disobeys the laws of life, "not one jot or tittle of which shall fail," either in exacting inevitable penalty for wrong living or in giving sure coming reward and crown for right or righteous living.

In every department of those giving recreation amusement to the public — the actor, the singer, the dancer, the acrobat, the circus rider, the athlete, the gymnast — are the laws of health, the means of securing and keeping the most vigor of mind and vigor of muscle, flexibility of mind and flexibility of muscle, more studied and practised, in proportion to numbers, than with any other class among us. For their art, their reputations, their incomes depend directly on their daily physical and mental condition. Neither physical or intellectual athlete can, for a single hour, delegate business to clerk, foreman, or overseer. It is their light which is expected to shine. Public admiration, appreciation and expectation are the most rigid of monitors in compelling the artist to travel in that straight and narrow path of temperance in all things, out of which to stray brings certain penalty of exhaustion and dimming of their light. Well, also, do these people know the increased strength, inspiration and clearness of mind that comes of keeping permanently in the calm, reposeful frame of mind, of avoiding moods of anger as sources of weakness, of fighting off the deadly sin of worry and fretfulness, knowing all this to be force expended in tearing themselves to pieces.

So in his eating and drinking, in all care and love for the health and vigor and elasticity of his body, to make it as perfect an instrument as possible for his higher unseen self to use, to act on, to act through, the artist, the actor, will, in Biblical phrase, "glorify God," glorify more and more that part of the infinite force which he or she represents.

The highest culture in any art will inevitably, as the laws governing growth in such art become more and more understood, lead any man or woman to take better care of their minds and bodies. The best care of the mind, the highest morality, the desire or aspiration for the thought freest from hate, envy, and low motive, will give the highest health, the greatest vigor, and the greatest genius.

The high priests of the drama, as of all art, are ever searching, desiring, reaching out for more power. Power of doing, and giving to others of what is done, is the grand attribute of deity. God is pictured as eternally serene, unruffled, calm, composed. The mind most free from *all* discordant, disturbed thought generates the most power. The drama depicting violence, bloodshed, torture, the drama of daggers, whether daggers of thought or daggers of steel, is not recreative. It stimulates, and that unhealthfully. It is of the same order of stimulation as that of the prize fight, the hanging, the spectacle of Christian captives torn to pieces by wild beasts, or any exhibition of combined physical and mental suffering to which thousands flock. It is not that a taste for murder and bloodshed is actually created by such exhibitions. You only bring to the front the old, savage instinct for blood or scenes of suffering innate in all of us more or less—the lingerings of cruder existences. A murder of any kind—a simulated murder—is an unhealthy exhibition, and has an unhealthy effect on him or her who exhibits. To act any character one must, for the time, BE that character,—be in the soul and spirit of the murder,—connect themselves temporarily with a murderous, violent, destructive, and hurtful current, element and atmosphere of thought, and this brings injury to mind and body.

As the race grows in refinement, it will take less and less pleasure in the drama which depicts death or suffering, or heart torture of any kind. **I am not seeking to " reform " the stage. I am not preaching** a crusade against any form of the present drama. People will have what they most want, and that as long as they want it. I doubt if any evil in the world was ever scolded out of existence. Scolding is only resisting one form of evil by fighting it with another— that other being the intemperance of hate, and hate often directed, not so much at the thing scolded at as the persons using that thing. But it is possible these opinions may find sympathy with some who have become wearied of dramatic vivisection tables. It partakes of the ghastly fancied to pay a dollar or two to see misery on the stage, when there's so much of the real article outside to be seen for nothing.

Why must there be a deadly, deep-dyed villain in so many dramas, a being incapable of goodness? Is it impossible to illustrate virtue, bravery, honesty, without a background of vice? Is it necessary to have a spoiled mackerel on the dinner-table to appreciate more keenly the savor and flavor of a fresh one?

The crying need and demand of our time is for more of real recreation. We are not a cheerful people. Thousands go home from work to mope or grumble. Look at the general expression on the faces of our crowds on car or ferry-boat, going to and returning from work. A smile, a cheerful face, a face good to look upon, is scarce. Glum, silent, serious, sour, but not always sober. There is not enough of the healthful stimulation of recreation. Lacking this, humanity runs to the unhealthy, artificial source of stimulation and temporary strength and cheer. Ten thousand barrooms supply it.

The force we call mind is always at work. It must

work. If you do not organize its forces it will work disorganized. The same force spent in idle lounging on a corner, can, otherwise directed, paint a picture or carve a statue, or admire the picture, or panorama, or scenic representation.

People do not want to see plays to be taught moral lessons. There are hard lessons enough outside in everybody's daily experience. We need plays, not so much to instruct as to amuse and rest brains. Rest a mind properly and it will instruct itself. It is innate in human nature to run away from a forced lesson. It is always a sign that the lesson is unattractive, — that somebody is teaching mechanically, perfunctorily, and with more of love for the pay than the effort. You put love in an art or in its teaching, and scholars will love to be taught. I sympathize now more than ever with the boy who runs away from school and takes to the woods. His running away is not a compliment to the teacher or the system, and is a compliment to the trees.

There has been, within the last ten or fifteen years, a great increase of the amateur element, so called. Its ability is marked, and is now recognized by the best mind of the profession. This supply comes in answer to a demand almost as yet unspoken for more recreation. It hardly knew the remedy. Yet the remedy is springing up on every side. It lies with the young people who desire to study for the stage. They are over all the land. There are places for them all, and channels for them all, if theirs is real **ability**. Love of art, for dramatic representation, **is increasing** its phases continually, and there are **ten eccentric** or individual characterizations where there was one thirty years ago. There is a mysterious law in nature which always brings the supply of a thing, or element or talent needed, before we really know that it is needed.

The drama, with its thousands of theatres, its tens of thousands of actors, its millions nightly filling its temples, should have its college equal in dignity and respectability to Yale or Harvard. That university should gather under one home roof the young men and women, who over all the land are wishing for dramatic and elocutionary training. It should grant a home and a protection for these young people, and such home should be presided over by a woman whose heart is in the work, and whose delight it would be to make the home for those who came to be educated.

There are few homes for the scholar in any of our colleges. There are boarding houses — sometimes mockeries of home, where the student is often made at home with all the annoyances of the family.

Home is the crowning effort, concentration and result of the highest culture and civilization, and of all places the school most needs it. Its education and influence goes beyond that of school or lecture room. That influence, that order of thought, that society most brought to bear upon you, when in the latter part of the day you are wearied and negative, and thereby easier to be swayed for good or ill, is of vast import for good or ill, and very often determines for good or ill the morals and fortunes of a young man or woman.

In the refined and ever refining home, education never stops. You create an atmosphere of refined thought, and all within its range are ever absorbing of such thought, be they at table or in the parlor; and where there is generated an atmosphere of tattle, scandal, littleness, narrowness, and envy, you absorb also of that contagion. It dims mind, diseases body, and negatives the effect of the best teachings of the class or lecture room. The coming dramatic university should have its theatre perfect in all appointments, its museum of costumes of all ages, its gymnasium, its lectures at intervals from those prominent in the professions, who could thus give suggestion founded on their individual experience and individual style. Receiving the sanction of the highest culture, its performances could be made remunerative. So could be the lectures given by prominent actors and actresses, and these in their preparation would derive benefit from a temporary change of occupation.

It should have also its own chapel, a chapel devoted to no one creed, but to all creeds; a chapel in architecture, painting and statuary, filled with symbolic representation of the highest and divinest idealizations; a chapel always open, where those so inclined could come and sit at all times, day or night, in silence — a place devoted to the sacred and mighty power of silent thought — a place to ask for and certainly receive what we all want, power; one place to which wisdom and inspiration, now known neither to earthly book or teacher, can be brought, and which, if you are receptive and teachable, and devout, you can and will receive; one place where the lower motive and sentiment of the world should not enter. For when you make a place like this, you open a door for higher intelligence than that seen of earth to come, and create an atmosphere where mind full of idea, wisdom, suggestion, relative to all that can advance human happiness and art, can come and drop thoughts like seeds in your minds. For it is only in silence, and by means of periods and places of silence, that the fullest force of the infinite and eternal mind can be by us felt and received.

The drama is rapidly asserting its worth, its use, and its dignity, and will repel every shade and approach of that social ostracism born and handed down of a barbaric era, when the man who could split the most skulls with the mace or sword took precedence of all other form of intellect; and wherever society today copies this sentiment, it copies a fashion first set by some mediæval royal bully, who designated the man who could write by the menial term "scrivener," and sat the priest at table with the servants.

VOICE OF THE MOUNTAIN.

Humanity still seeks to climb heavenward,
Up Babel towers of swarded wealth,
And still is blind to that Great Law
Which discord, strife, confusion sends amid the workers
As monitors to show God must be trusted,
Not fought with barricades of bank safes.

    For him that trusts, the world is his,
    Skies, mountains, clouds, birds, trees, and flowers,
Lakes, streams, storms, calms, crowded cities, empty
    wastes,
All cry to him "Enjoy!"
Solitude, the vulgar's dread, becomes his inspiration.
The mountains nurse him,
With Deity upon their tops oft he renews his covenant —
Nor needs for other company.
Babble there of common things to him is blasphemy!
Sublimer even than the thunder's roll
Is Shasta's icy silence,
Brooding over past eternities,
When present sun and system were unborn;
When naught was save the Great I Am!
Before whom earth's age and history to atom dwindles.
So to Him speak the Sierras,
Ever pointing with fingers, storm-worn and scarred,
Beyond all time, and space, and thought,

Beyond all law, all plan, all theory,
Pointing to that void, terrible, unknown and inconceivable,
Never to be lit up,
Without beginning, ending, bounds or history.

Here man fears God,
At once his littleness and greatness feels —
Little that he's an atom of the infinite mystery —
Great that he's a part of Infinite Divinity.

This is the voice of the mountains!
Nor what men call learning, nor culture, nor civilization are needed to know its meaning.
Often it speaks loudest to unlettered men.
The Indian hears it plainer than we;
He is content to live only that he may hear it.
He cares not for ships, nor roads, nor arts, nor commerce,
Nor the heaping up of gold,
Nor to babble, or prate, or preach;
Content with what nature sends him.
As a child the father, so he trusts the Great Spirit.

A few hear this voice!
God has moulded and fashioned them,
He has singled them out and beckoned them to follow Him into the wilderness,
He has effaced their likeness to common men,
He has for them placed thorns in every broad road, that they shall walk in the straight and narrow path;
And when they hear His voice,
When all that was and is, and is to be, ever murmurs in their ears,
With a mighty sound which is yet a mighty silence,
Then are they ready to speak to men.

VOICE OF THE MOUNTAIN.

   Their lives are as new books,
Open for all worthy to read.
Open, honest, impulsive, impassioned lives —
Nature trusted in the sight of men.
Thought, passion, sentiment, the evil and the good, the
  gold and the dross,
All openly displayed;
They are as living sermons, more potent than pulpit
  homilies.

THE USES OF SICKNESS.

Copyright, 1888, by F. J. Needham.

In this era of our planet's existence, there can scarcely be for anyone entire escape from ills of the body. But there are two entirely different methods of treating in mind those states of the body we call sickness. The right one is to consider and hold in mind, and ever desire earnestly, that you may be led into more and more faith that all pain, sickness, and debility, of whatever nature, are but efforts of the spirit to purge itself, and throw off from the body that which has become too gross for your spirit to use.

Here bear in mind the fact which it is necessary often to repeat, that your spirit is one thing and your body quite another; that your spirit is an ever-increasing power, the growth of ages, and that your body is only its temporary instrument, for use in this one present phase of existence.

We are ever liable to glide unconsciously into the old belief in which we have been educated, that all there is of us is the physical body. Without the spirit, the body is only the engine, without steam to move it.

An ever-increasing realization that spirit and body are two distinct things, and that the spirit is the only moving, building, and working force for the body, will prove a great help to your spirit to act favorably on the body, and reconstruct it anew.

The second wrongful and injurious method of using sickness, is to hold and firmly believe that you are nothing but the body you use; that it is only the body which is sick; that its only cure lies in material remedies; that its present state of sickness or debility is but an unmitigated evil, and not the means whereby it is being freed from a load of relatively dead matter, too lifeless and inert for the spirit to use. This indicates utter ignorance of the spirit; and such ignorance of the spirit brings on more and more of disease and corporeal deadness, until at last your real and only power, your spirit, is unable to carry the half dead body any longer. It frees itself from such encumbrance. You call that death. It is only the dropping of a load by the spirit, too heavy longer to be carried.

There are in the world today many people who are already half dead. In other words, their spirits do but half carry their bodies. The stooping shoulders, bent knees, feeble gait, and general failing senses of a man or woman at the age of sixty, are so many evidences that the mind using that body is in utter ignorance of its power to recuperate and regenerate that body. All that power through its character of belief is now being used to destroy the body. If the mind is in the right belief, the body will come out of its trial purified of grossness, more refined, more active and stronger than ever. In the physical sense, it has grown younger instead of older.

Even if you can but entertain and give this idea a respectful hearing, it will make a great difference for the better out of your physical ill. Because, in even changing to this extent the attitude of your mind, you have opened a door for your higher self to work for good upon the body. Belief in the truth will then help the mind to more command over the body. Command of mind over body must ultimately free the body from every ill and pain. The physical trials you may now pass through are not always to be necessary in the purging and refining process. These first trials are the hardest. As the spirit gains more and more supremacy and faith in these truths, which will be more and more proven, the body will pass through the changes incident to the growing power of the spirit with less and less pain and inconvenience.

If you receive a new and truthful idea, it will work a change in the body. Your present muscle, blood and bone are all material expressions of, and physical correspondences of, your prevailing order of thought. Change that thought, and a change must take place in the character and quality of the seen material forming the body. If the unseen power of the body is changed, that which is seen must change.

Such changes, to a limited extent, are constantly at work in daily life. Give a person in despair or discouragement, hope, or promise of something better, and a change in the body is soon manifest. The eye grows brighter, the muscles are braced **more** firmly, and every movement shows more **vigor. A** new element of thought is not only **acting on that** body, but has actually entered into and assimilated with it.

On the contrary, throw a thought of terror suddenly into the mind, and such is the effect of that thought-element acting on the body and actually entering into the composition of the body, that, as known in varying instances, faces grow pale, knees totter, weakness succeeds strength, digestion is checked, insensibility is sometimes brought on, the hair has bleached in a few hours, and even instant death has been thereby caused.

The terrifying cry of "Fire!" in a crowded theatre, the cry of alarm raised in a crowd of people, brings an element and a force to act first on the minds, and next on the bodies of those people, which, though unseen, is as real, in a material sense, as is any noxious gas or vapor, like the fumes of burning charcoal, which, though unseen, proves its existence by its fatal results.

All pain comes of the effort of the spirit to force new life into a part of the body lacking life. Or it comes of the spirit's effort to throw off altogether such part lacking life, and replace it with new material. In cases when the spirit ceases from such effort, there comes cessation from pain and insensibility, the forerunner of the body's death.

When disease is regarded in what we will here call the remedial light, life assumes an entirely new aspect. The life of the body becomes then a succession of rebirths or changes from coarser to finer material, each birth or change being less painful than the one preceding, until, at last, such change is accompanied only by a period of languor and physical inactivity. Or, in other words, the spirit is making the body into its own image, so that it shall be the perfect instrument to carry out its desires. Then body and spirit are wedded. They are as one.

If the mind or spirit in ignorance accepts implicitly these old errors, then that mind is already sick, though the body it uses is strong. If the mind is sick, the body in time must become sick. But when the awakened mind refuses any longer to accept these old errors, and desires that it may come to know and reject all other error, of which it may now be unconscious, that mind is relatively healthy. It is then on the road to higher and higher health. True, its body may for periods be prostrated through the changes, which a change from lower to higher mental conditions will bring about. But such periods of physical ailment become as ends to a higher health, because the mind, being in the right direction, is pushing the body in that direction, whereas the mind in ignorance, not having the vestige of an idea that it is the power which rules the body, accepts blindly the error which the body in a sense teaches it, and then uses all its force to build on and increase that error. The body used and ruled by such a mind will have disease in its worst form, until such body is at last destroyed. The body used and ruled by the mind inclined in the right direction may have ailment and suffer, but it will, if the faith of its spirit has grown strong enough, come out of the trial purified, refined, strengthened, and having **more** power than ever to resist evil and prevent **the absorp-**

tion from lower minds of their lower and injurious thought, which to the sensitive person is a prolific source of disease.

In many cases, through natural birth, the spirit is given a body with which it is at total variance. That body may come into the world freighted with a certain mind of its own. That mind comes of the lower and erroneous thought absorbed in gestation, infancy, and youth. That lower mind may rule the body for years, or for its whole physical lifetime. The real self, the real spirit, may only influence what may be called a fragment of that body, and this only at certain periods favorable to its access. The lower mind may rule much of the time with low and gross desires. For the whole thought-current of the lower or "carnal mind" rules on this stratum of life, and meets the higher mind with obstacles or temptation at every point.

For such a spirit even to preserve at all its present body, may involve much pain and sickness. This comes of the war betwixt spirit and body. The spirit seeks to fashion the body in accord with itself, and tries to throw off the old dead thought in which the body has been educated. The body resists. The body has an individuality of its own. It desires to preserve that individuality. It feels in the effort of the spirit not only an invasion of such individuality, but an attempt to destroy that individuality forever. This is actually the case. If the individuality of the body is one of error and belief in untruth, it cannot last. It must be destroyed. Nothing can endure permanently but what is based in truth. Sickness, then, is a means for the removal of the old body, exactly as when you make a new wall of an old one, by taking away, piecemeal, portions of the old, replacing them with new and sound material, until the wall is altogether new.

There may be nothing new under the sun, but there are things innumerable, now unknown, which would be new to us. We have touched hardly the edge of our real life, and know little what it means really to live.

Nor can we take in at once much of what is new without danger. Truth must be received in small doses, otherwise a sudden flood of light, a sudden revelation of life's possibilities, would cause so sudden a physical change, and so great a disturbance betwixt spirit and body, as possibly to destroy the body. The removal of the old, and its replacement by the new, should be a gradual process. It is akin to digestion. Too much food taken at once into the stomach brings pain and disturbance. Too much of new idea taken at once, is the putting of new wine into old bottles. The old bottle represents the old body, the new wine is new thought. All idea is actual force; and if more force be received than the old body can appropriate, there is a possibility that its working will burst the bottle.

The new material given you by this change is new and true thought or idea. That will materialize blood, bone, muscle, and nerve into a newer, finer, and stronger quality of seen substance.

A child bred in the belief that its real self is **only the body it uses, that there is no power behind that** body, which, if known and rightly directed, can ever rehabilitate it with new element, recuperate it, and ever make its material substance over and over again, each time newer, finer, and stronger, such a child — and many such there now are — not only has within it what may be termed the "seeds of disease," but through its total ignorance, combined with the ignorance of other minds about it, nearly all the power of its spirit is worked the wrong way — worked to feed and strengthen disease, and so, at last, make the body unbearable for the spirit.

There is a kind and quality of mind affecting us all more or less. It is sometimes called the "unconscious mind." It is belief in error, absorbed from others possibly in infancy and youth, which we have never questioned and never doubted — never thought to question or doubt, and which we blindly go on believing, scarcely knowing it is our belief. But such belief affects us for good or ill, just as much as that of which we are conscious of believing.

Holding such unconscious error today, thousands of hearty, athletic young men, now in the fullest possession of vigor and muscular strength, believe that at the age of fifty this vigor must begin to lessen, and that between sixty or seventy, some "ill that flesh is heir to" must necessarily beset them, and ultimately carry them off. To say to them, seriously, that a time is coming when man's superior knowledge will enable him to keep his body as long as he pleases, and in an ever-improving condition, would immediately call from them either ridicule or that obstinate incredulity which will not for one moment entertain a new idea as a possibility.

Nothing is more dangerous than that permanent state of mind which instantly rejects and refuses for one moment to entertain, hospitably, a new idea, because it seems to that mind wild, unreasonable, and visionary. It is the same condition which in years by-gone scornfully rejected steam and electricity as "new-fangled notions." It is the condition which makes for itself a rut of thought and occupation, and travels round and round in it without any advance forward to newer life and possibilities. It is the condition leading surely to fossilization of both mind and body.

Thousands are today unconsciously imprisoned in the idea that what all human or physical life has been in the past, that it must necessarily be in the future, and that it must necessarily involve the three periods of youth, maturity, and decay. To believe this so implicitly, makes these phases of life inevitable for the believer, and bars the door against any new possibilities.

Flesh is heir to no ills save those bequeathed the flesh by the spirit in ignorance. The spirit once in the truth can bequeath the flesh only more and more life; in brief, "life everlasting."

Do you ask what are some of the errors unconsciously held by thousands about us? An individual whom you know to be a demagogue or charlatan, passes with thousands as a great man. A system of education which you know to be honey-combed with falsity and the blind repetition of custom, they accept as perfect. War between nations which you know to be but blind idiocy, they accept as a "political necessity," because from infancy the sound of those two words has been trumpeted into their ears and remains clinched there. Customs, usages, and habits, which you know to be not only useless, but resulting in injury or inconvenience, are perpetuated from generation to generation, unthought of, unquestioned.

The cruelty wantonly inflicted by our race on beast and bird in their natural state, in slaughtering and mutilating them for mere amusement, as well as the imprisonment of every species of biped and quadruped, dooming the inhabitants of field, forest, and air to an unnatural and suffering life, simply that we may stare at them behind their bars, is another evidence of the unconsciousness of our race to the wrong and injustice which it permits, and even endorses as right and proper.

The degraded estimation in which woman is held by great masses of men; the degraded estimation which she accepts without question or protest herself; the estimate of her by so many men, either as a pleasing toy or a convenience; the ignorance and denial by most men that she is equal to him in power for business or any pursuit, as well as the ignorance and consequent denial, both on his or her part, that she is, when rightly understood, a necessary factor to his highest success,— all these are still unconscious errors leading to grevious ills in the minds of millions on millions.

The still prevailing ignorance that thought is an element and force, working results miles from the body it uses; that every thought or idea of ours is like an unseen magnet, which, if held to, will bring to us in material things the likeness of that thought; the common idea that it matters little what we think, so long as our thought is not known; the ignorance that what we think of others and ourselves has everything to do with our health and fortunes, for happiness or misery; the sloughs of physical misery and mental disturbance, into which so many plunge themselves unconsciously, through association with minds lower than theirs, and so absorbing and living in such lower thought; the ignorance that every individual has lived in the past other lives, and must in the future live more, either with or without a body, — all these form but a fragment of the unconscious errors prevalent all about us. For the mind ever calling for more truth and light, every bodily trial results in a greater and greater awakening to these and hundreds of other errors, which, so long as held in mind, bring inevitably results in pain and misery to us.

"The truth shall make you free," says the biblical record. It is so. The truth shall free us from every form of physical and mental suffering; and when the God in yourself rules completely the old and lower self, all tears are then wiped from our eyes.

PRENTICE MULFORD.

MUSEUM AND MENAGERIE HORRORS.

A MENAGERIE of beasts and birds means a collection of captured walking and flying creatures, taken from their natural modes of life, deprived permanently of such modes, and suffering more or less in consequence. The bird, used to the freedom of forest and air, is imprisoned in the most limited quarters. Its plumage there is never as fresh and glossy as in its natural state. It does not live as long. The captive life of the many specimens brought from the tropics is very short, especially of the smaller and more delicate species.

Bears, lions, tigers, deer, wolves and all other animals like liberty and freedom of range as well as man. In the menagerie they are deprived of it. The air they breathe is often fetid and impure. To the burrowing animal, earth is as much a necessity and comfort as a comfortable bed is to us. The captured burrower is often kept on a hard board floor, which, in its restless misery to get into its native earth, it scratches and wears away in cavities inches in depth.

Monkeys by the thousand die prematurely of consumption, because forced to live in a climate too cold and damp for them, and no amount of artificial heat can supply the element to which they have been accustomed in the air of their native tropic groves and jungles.

Seals are kept in tanks of fresh water, when salt water is their natural element. Their captive lives are always short.

There is no form of organized life but that is a part and belonging of the locality and latitude where in its wild state it is born. The polar bear is a natural belonging of the Arctic regions. The monkey is a belonging and outgrowth of tropical conditions. When either of these are taken from climes native to them, and out of which they do not voluntarily wander, pain is inflicted on them.

Go to the cheap "museum," now so plentiful, and regard the bedraggled plumage and apparent sickly condition of many of the birds, natives of distant climes, imprisoned there. You see them but for an hour. Return in a few months and you will not find them. What has become of them. They have died, and their places are supplied by others likewise slowly dying. The procession of captives so to suffer and die prematurely never ceases moving into these places. Ships are constantly bringing them hither. An army of men distributed all over the world, and ranging through the forests of every clime, is constantly engaged in trapping them. For what reasons are all these concentrations of captured misery, now to be found in every large town and city of our country? Simply to gratify human curiosity. Simply that we may stand a few minutes and gaze at them behind their bars. What do we then learn of their real natures and habits in these prisons? What would be learned of your real tastes, inclinations and habits were you kept constantly in a cage?

Is the gratification of this curiosity worth the misery it costs?

If a bird wooed by your kindness comes and builds its nest in a tree near your window, and there rears its brood, is not the sight it affords from day to day worth a hundred times more than that of the same bird, deprived of its mate and shut up in a cage? Will you not, as in its freedom you study its real habits and see its real and natural life, feel more and more drawn to it by the tie of a common sympathy, as you see evidenced in that life so much that belongs to your own? Like you, it builds a home; like you, it has affection and care for its mate; like you, it provides for its family; like you, it is alarmed at the approach of danger; like you, it nestles in the thought of security.

Yet so crude and cruel still is the instinct in our race, that the ruin of the wild bird's home, or its slaughter or capture, is the ruling desire with nineteen boys out of twenty as they roam the woods; and "cultured parents" will see their children leave the house equipped with the means for this destruction without even the thought of protest.

WHO ARE OUR RELATIONS?

COPYRIGHT, 1888, BY F. J. NEEDHAM.

The man or woman who is most like you in tastes, motives, and habits of thought, and to whom you feel most attracted, may not be brother, sister, cousin, or any physical relative at all. But such person is to you a very near relation.

Your brothers or sisters may not be like you at all in mind, taste, and inclination. You may associate with them because they are members of the family, but were you not to know them as brothers, sisters, or other relatives, or were you to see elsewhere their exact counterparts in character, you might not like such counterparts at all.

Physical or "blood relationship" has very little bearing on the real or mental relationship. It is possible for a brother or sister, a father or mother to be very closely allied to you in thought and sympathy. Again, it is possible for a father or mother, brother or sister, to be very remote from you in thought and sympathy, and to live in a realm or atmosphere of thought very unlike yours.

You can live neither healthfully or comfortably, unless with those whose thought-atmosphere (a literal emanation from them) is similar to your own. Physical relationship may or may not furnish such atmosphere. Compel a laboring man, whose thought goes little beyond his eating, drinking and daily round of work, to live exclusively with a company of artists and philosophers, seeing none of his own kind and order of thought, and that man's spirits would in time be depressed, and his health would suffer. The same law works when the superior mind is compelled to constant association with the inferior. Such may be your position among physical relatives.

Children live, thrive, and are exhilarated by the thought-atmosphere emanating from their playmates. Cut them entirely off from such association and they droop. As a child, you lived upon this atmosphere of childhood; that is, you lived in the spiritual relationship of childhood, and regarding a certain playful thought nutriment, received it and also gave it to your playmates. You may wonder now why you cannot arouse the old feeling and exhilaration coming either from the associations of childhood or youth. It is because your spirit requires another thought food or atmosphere, which only another, and probably higher order of mind can give. That received, and time would pass as quickly and pleasantly as it did with the associates of your earlier physical existence.

Those who can furnish it are your real relations. But such relationship cannot exist unless you can furnish them with the same quality of thought in return.

The real or spiritual relations of many merchants, mechanics, and those of other callings, are their brother merchants, mechanics, or those of similar occupations. They prove this by their lives. They feel more at home with those whose business is like their own than they do in the places they may call home, to which they resort to eat, sleep, and spend often a tiresome Sunday, longing for Monday's coming, and the more welcome life of the market-stall and store. Because there they are amongst their real relations, and are being literally fed and stimulated by the thought-atmosphere furnished them by these relatives, which they also furnish in turn.

Every order of mind or quality of thought must have association with a corresponding order of mind and quality of thought, or it will suffer. But "blood relationship" has little to do with furnishing such order of thought.

There is a vast amount of unconscious tyranny exercised through the ties of physical relationship. Children often, when grown up, place the mothers or fathers in their minds in a sphere and method of life where they may or may not care to belong. Then thought, seldom if ever expressed, runs in substance thus: "Mother is getting too old to wear bright colors. She must dress more subdued." "It is ridiculous for mother (if a widow) to marry again" (very hard cash reasons sometimes entering into this sentiment). "Mother, of course, does not want to enter into our gayer life, so she can stay at home and take care of the children." Or, "It is time father retired from busines," or, "Father's idea of marrying again is ridiculous."

No force is more subtle in its workings, nor more powerful to bring results for good or ill than the steady output of thought from one or several minds combined, on one person to effect some desired result, and whether this is done intelligently and consciously, or blindly, the force works the same result.

Now a continual flow of this kind of thought, coming from, possibly, three or four minds to whom "mother" was instrumental in furnishing new bodies, and continually directed on "mother," is a very powerful force to direct and keep her exactly where the children find it most convenient to have her. The whole conventional current of thought also flows as an aid in this direction. "Mother," says this unspoken sentiment, "must of course grow old, retire gradually from a more active and gayer life, and retire also to a corner of the household, to associate with other shelved and declining parents, and be useful as a general upper nurse in times of sickness or other family emergency." Through the action on her of these minds, many mothers cease to have any privileges as individuals, and eventually do exactly as their children desire.

Possibly it is here remarked or thought, "But should I not go to my mother or other near relative with my cares and trials, and receive her help, as I have always been in the habit of doing? Ought not those of my own family, above all others, to help me in time of need?"

Certainly, if the mother or any of your physical relatives are glad and anxious so to do. Certainly, if such service from a relative comes directly from the heart, and is not impelled by the sentiment taking sometimes this form of unspoken expression:

"I suppose I must do this because it is my brother, or my son, or other physical relative who asks it." Asks it? Many, many are these services which are unconsciously demanded, rather than asked, in these cases. Loads are piled upon relatives simply *because* they are relatives. Favors in money — in the indorsement of notes, are in a sense exacted through sympathy of relatives. Support, food, shelter, maintenance, are expected from relatives when it cannot be procured elsewhere. Hospitality is *expected* from relatives, when to expect hospitality is to make such entertainment the result of a demand. Presents are expected from relatives, when to expect a gift makes it rather an extortion.

Real gifts are always surprises. No one expects a surprise, since expectation destroys surprise.

Relatives visit and "camp down" on other relatives simply because they are relatives, and a vast amount of grudging, grumbling, but unspoken thought, is always going out when relatives use each other's houses to save hotel bills.

No real or lasting good comes of any gift bestowed on another unless the heart goes with it, and its bestowal is to the giver an act of unalloyed pleasure. Because something else goes with the material gift, the food, the shelter, the loan, which, though not seen, and little known, is more important than the gift itself. That is the thought which goes with it. That thought strongly affects, for good or ill, the person who receives the gift. If, as giving within your means, you bestow the merest trifle in **money** upon a person in need, and the thought **that goes** with it is not only the most sincere desire to help that person, but you feel a keen sense of pleasure in giving such help, then you throw upon that person a certain thought-element which will never leave them, and benefit them eternally and in proportion to the quality, power and force of your thought. Then you do far more than relieve their present physical necessity. You give them a certain amount of spiritual power. Your wish that their power may be so developed and increased as to enable them to live above beggary, and draw to themselves the goods of this earth (as all will and must, when grown to a certain stature in spiritual power), is a great help for them in time to acquire such power. You have sent and sown in them a seed of thought which will take root and bear fruit at some period of their real or spiritual existence.

But if you give grudgingly, if you give under any sort of compulsion, if you give food, shelter, clothing, money, anything, only because circumstances compel you so to do, or because people might talk unfavorably of you for not giving, or because other people are so giving, then your gift does relatively little good, no matter on whom bestowed, be it even mother, father, brother, sister, son or daughter.

You relieve, then, only a physical necessity, and that only for a time. You may possibly feed a body, shelter it, clothe it. But you do not, and cannot feed properly the spirit that uses that body if the thought going with your gift is not that of the most perfect willingness and hearty pleasure in relieving that body's necessities. The grudging thought accompanying the gift, the thought common to that position when the recipient of the gift (no matter how near the relationship) is endured rather than enjoyed, the thought accompanying any gift to any person, or relative, that it is given principally because custom and public opinion require it, or because of the recipient's importunity, is a great damage both to giver and taker. It is the sending to the one who receives a current of thought, evil in its character and result. It brings back to the giver from the one who takes a response in thought of like nature, and this also is harmful. Because, if you receive a gift which you have in any way extorted, your feeling for the giver is not that of warm, glowing gratitude, but something quite different.

The Christ of Judea, when commending the widow who cast her mite into the treasury, did so in our estimation and as seen in this light, not merely because she gave in proportion to her material means, but because he saw that her thought of desire to help in whatever way help was needed, going with that mite, was far more heartfelt and genuine than that of richer people who cast in larger sums, but cast in also with them a lower character of thought and motive. He saw, also, that the woman's thought was actually doing far more to help than that of the others, for it was purer, less mixed with lower motive, and therefore far the stronger.

"Is it not my duty," some may ask, "to feed, clothe, shelter, and support a very near relative or parent, if helpless, in their old age?

The term "doing from a sense of duty" **does not**

always imply that the thing done, be it the person helped or the patient nursed through sickness, is done from the impulse of love for that person or love for the doing. It is sometimes done mechanically, or with dislike for the doing. It is sometimes a forced and painful performance. For such reason little good is done, for if physical necessities are temporarily relieved, spiritual necessities are not, and unless the spiritual portion of our natures is fed, there can be no permanent relief or good done the physical. Parents who in old age are supported by their children merely from a sense of duty, have sometimes their spirits wounded and starved — wounded, because they feel they are endured incumbrances — starved, because no real love goes with the gift or service done by these children. Children who come into the world unwelcomed by the parent and are brought up only because custom, conventionality and public opinion demands their support from that parent, are most unfortunate, and suffer from the blight and starvation thereby caused their spirits. Genuine heartfelt love is literally life giving, and if received by the child is for it a source of cheer, health, strength, and activity.

There is a certain trained conscience whose basis of education is fear of public or private opinion. This sometimes really impels acts which are said to be done from a "sense of duty." If public opinion should suddenly change, and cast no censure at all on the person who refused to support very near relatives in want or old age, a proportion of such relatives would probably go to the poor-house, and the son or daughter who sent them there would be acting out their real natures, and not feigning a sentiment they did not possess.

Mothers sometimes say, "I don't care what becomes of me, so that my children are well brought up and educated." A mother should care a great deal for her own cultivation. If her cultivation and growth in wisdom is checked, that of her children will be checked. It will be checked if she sinks herself in her endeavor to favor her children. A genuine mother will continually compel the admiration and respect, as well as love of her children. Such admiration and respect can be compelled only by a woman who knows the world, has standing and position in it, and is ever pushing forward to more commanding place and position. Such admiration and respect from son or daughter cannot be compelled by the mother who retires to a household corner, becomes a cross between upper nurse and governess, neglects her dress and personal appearance, and teaches her children that she is at their disposal and use, in all family emergencies, real or fancied. For this very reason are many mothers run over, snubbed, and ridiculed by their grown-up children.

If mothers so sink themselves, as they falsely imagine, to benefit their children, they pay in cases a terrible penalty. If you allow your will constantly to be overborne by another; if you give up your own preferences and inclinations, and become only another's echo; if you live about as others desire, you will lose more and more, for this existence, the power of self-assertion; you will absorb so much of the other mind and thought about you as to become a part of that mind, and so act in accordance even with its silent will and unspoken desire; you will fossilize, and sink into a hopeless servitude; you will lose more and more of both physical and mental power for doing anything; you will become the chimney-corner encumbrance, the senile parent, the helpless old man or woman, endured rather than loved.

This, in many instances, has been the effect of the grown-up children's minds upon a parent.

It is the silent force of those minds, continually working on that of the parent, that helps to break the parent down physically, and the decay and mental weakness, commonly charged to "advancing years," is due in part to the injurious effect of a mind or group of minds, seeking to usurp and overpower another. This evil is done unconsciously. The son wishes to manage the farm. His will may be strong. He gains power step by step. He takes as rights what at first he took only by the father's permission or as privileges. He goes on step by step, having his way in all things, great and small, perhaps being aided by others of the children, using their silent force in the same direction. And this may be a combined force almost impossible for one person to withstand, if continually exposed to it. It is a steady, incessant pressure, all in one direction. It works night and day. It works all the more efficaciously, because the parent so exposed to it is utterly ignorant of such a force and its operation upon him. He finds himself growing weak. He becomes inert.

He lacks his old vigor, and thinks it is through the approach of old age.

I knew a man over seventy years of age and as sound, active and vigorous in mind and body as one of forty. He had organized and built up a large business. His several children at last took it into their heads that it was time "father retired from business." Henceforth, the thought spoken and unspoken, bearing month in and month out on father from the children, was this desire and demand that he should retire from business. Confiding his situation to a friend, he said, "Why should I retire from business? I live in it, I like it, and so far as I can see, am able to conduct it properly." But the persistent demand and force brought to bear on him from these foes of his own blood and household was too great to withstand. He did retire. The sons and daughters were satisfied. The father soon commenced to decline in health. He lived about two years afterward, and one of his last remarks was, "My children have killed me."

"Ought I not to love my children above all others?" asks one.

The term "ought" has no application to the nature of love. Love goes where it will, and to whom it will, and where it is attracted. You cannot force yourself to love anything or anybody. There have been parents who had no real love for their children, and children who had no real love for their parents. Neither party can be blamed for this. They **were** lacking in the capacity for loving. They were **born** so lacking. They are no more to be **censured for** such deficiency than you would censure a person for being born blind or a cripple.

Some parents fancy they love their children, yet do not. A father who loses his temper and beats his son does not really love that son. It would be better to say that he loved to beat him, or tyrannize over him. Government in the family is necessary; but no sound, loving government is administered on a basis of anger and irascibility. Parents sometimes interfere and seriously affect the future of a child by opposing its desires in the choice of a profession. The parent may be prejudiced against certain walks in life. The child may wish to follow one of these walks. It meets a bitter, uncompromising opposition on the parent's part. There is no reasoning, discussion, or counselling in the matter — nothing but a stern, positive "No." Such sentiment and act are not impelled by love for the child on the parent's part. They are impelled by the parent's love for his or her own opinion and a love of tyranny. Parents sometimes forget that after the child emerges from the utter physical and mental helplessness of infancy, it is becoming more and more an individual. As an individual it may show decided tastes, preferences and inclinations in some direction. No parent and no person can break or alter these tastes and preferences. No one can make that child's mind over into something else. For the child's mind, as we call it, is really a mind or spirit, which has lived other physical lives from infancy to maturity, if not to old age, and as it comes into possession of its new body, and acquires a relative control over that body, it will begin to act out the man or woman as it was in its former life, and that may be a man or woman very closely related to the parent, or hardly related at all. But in any event, the parent is dealing with an individual, who is growing more and more into tastes, preferences, and traits of character which belong to and are a part of it. These *must* have expression. They will have expression in mind or spirit, whether allowed to physically or not. If the boy is ever longing to go to sea, and the parent forbids, the boy is on the sea in mind; and if so in mind, it is far better that his body should follow, for there is only damage when mind and body are not working in correspondence together. If the mother refuse to allow the boy to go to sea because she fears its dangers for him, still she is loving her own fears and her own way, too, more than she does her son.

The parent sometimes usurps a complete tyranny, not only over the child's body, but over its mind. The child's tastes, inclination, tendencies and preferences are held as of no importance whatever. If the boy wants to be a sailor, and the parent wants him something else — that something else the parent may insist that he shall be, but does he succeed? Let the host of mediocrity in all callings in the land answer. And mediocrity means the mechanical following of any pursuit in which there is no live interest.

More than this; where a body is compelled to do one thing, or live in a certain way, and the mind longs to live in another, there is a force set in motion which in many cases tears mind and body **apart**; and parents sometimes grieve over the loss of a child, when they are responsible for the death of its body from this cause.

How long, then, should parental control continue over the child — or, rather, over a spirit for which you have been an agency for furnishing with a new body.

Is it unreasonable to say that such control should not continue after such body, emerging from the helplessness of infancy, shall have acquired such control of its organization as shall enable it to meet all physical demands and necessities? To go beyond this, and give food, clothes, shelter, maintenance, to a person, is doing him or her a great injustice, and even cruelty. In so doing, you do not grant exercise to those faculties which must be used in coping successfully with the world. You make the children the less fitted to be self-sustaining, and earn their own living. You teach them to lie in a soft, luxurious bed, when they should be out in the world exercising and making more strong and dexterous their powers, both of mind and body.

Parents sometimes make themselves unjustly responsible, and inflict needless mental suffering on themselves, for the errors and tendencies of their children. A son or daughter takes a wrong course — or, rather, let us put it, a course where the evil is more prominent or more opposed to conventional ideas of propriety than other habits, more tolerated and deemed reputable, but which may be the subtle, and for the most part unknown, sources of as great ills as those condemned by society. A son takes to drink or reckless associates and commits some crime. The parent condemns herself for not having looked more carefully after her boy. She may accuse herself as having been, through her neglect, the prime agency for her son's misdeeds.

Madame, you blame yourself far too much. You did not make that son or daughter's character. It was made long before that spirit had the use of its last new body. What traits, what imperfections were very prominent in its last existence, will appear in its next. If that was a thieving spirit before, it will probably show thieving tendencies now. If it was gross, animal and gluttonous, then similar tendencies will show themselves now. You, if grown to a more refined plane of thought, may do much to modify and lessen these tendencies.

But all that you will do in this respect will be done through the silent force and action of your superior thought on your child's mind. It will not be done through a great deal of verbal counsel or physical punishment or discipline.

Whatever a mind is on entering on a new physical experience, whatever imperfection belongs to it, must appear and be acted out and beget pain and punishment of some kind, until that spirit sees clearly for itself, how, through its errors, it brings these punishments on itself. These lessons can only be learned when that person has full freedom, so far as parental control goes, to live as it pleases. You may for a time control such a life, and make it externally live as you please. But such external life is only a veneer, if the mind be full of lower tastes and inclinations. The sooner these are lived out, the sooner will that person learn the real law, which inflicts pains and penalties for breaking its unchangeable rules, and the sooner will it know the happiness which comes of living in accordance with its rules. That every spirit must do for him or herself.

A parent may mould a false character for a child. It may teach indirectly, through the effect of its own mental condition operating on the child, how to feign what the world calls goodness, how it may seem as regards outward conduct, to be what it is not at all in secret tendency and inclination, — how, in brief, to be a hypocrite.

No person is really reformed by another, in the sense such a term is sometimes used. Reform must come from within. It must be self-sustaining. It must not depend wholly on another's presence or influence. If it does, it is only a temporary reform. It will fail when the influence of the person on whom it depends is removed. We hear sometimes the assertion, "such or such a person's wife has been the making of him" (meaning the husband). By the way, why do we never hear of the man's being the making of his wife?

A man may be prevented from intemperance, or he may continually be braced up to meet the world through his wife's influence and mental power. But if in such reform he relies entirely upon her; if he cannot sustain himself without her continual presence and prompting, his is no lasting reformation, and he is also a very heavy and damaging load for her to carry. It is a one-sided piece of business when one person must supply all the sustaining force for two, and if this is persisted in, the wife, or whoever so supplies it, will at last sink under such burthen, and there will be two wrecked lives instead of one. No person can "make another," in the highest sense. But one person having the superior mind, can, if in a very close and long-continued association with one weaker, give temporarily to the weaker their very life and force, if their desire is very strong to help the weaker. If it be the husband who so receives of the wife, and is so dependent on the wife, then he does not represent any character of his own. He represents and is clothed temporarily with his wife's character, or as much of it as he can appropriate. If she dies, or is removed from him, then he relapses and sinks into his real self, unless he is resolved to be self-sustaining, and evolve force out of himself instead of using another's. If she continues to supply him, she is only sustaining his temporary character, which cannot last when its source of supply is removed, and in such continuance she will certainly in time exhaust herself.

Parents often unconsciously teach their children to lie down upon them, to depend upon them too long for moral support. The result of this error is that when the parent's life is dragged out, through carrying so heavy a load, the child ceases to have any genuine love for its parent. You may pity what is decrepit, weak, and shattered. Love it you cannot. Love is based on admiration, and admiration is not compelled by decay.

The tendency called instinct, which **impels** the

mother bird to turn its young out of the nest, so soon as they have sufficient strength to fly, and the animal in weaning its young to turn them adrift and leave them to shift for themselves, is founded on the natural and divine laws. We may say it is the custom of the brutes, and is therefore "brutal." But would it be a kindness for the bird to encourage the young to stay in the nest, where it could not gain strength, and when a few weeks will bring the storms and severity of winter, which the parent bird itself cannot withstand? Again, the parent, be it bird, animal, or human mother, needs after these periods of bringing their young into the world and rearing them, a season of entire rest and recuperation, and the duration of such resting season should be proportionate to the complexity of the organization and the force expended by such organization. During such periods, the parent should be freed from any and all demands from the child. Birds and animals in their natural or wild life take such periods of rest. But thousands of human mothers are never free from the demands of their children, until worn out they drop into their graves. They should be as free, so far as their children are concerned, as they were in girlhood, and before they became mothers. Motherhood is a most necessary and an indispensable phase of existence for ripening and developing qualities. But no one experience should be followed and dwelt in forever. Life in its more perfected state will be full of alternations — not a rut, into which if you are once set you must continually travel.

If human children remain with the mother for years after attaining what may be termed a responsible age; if they always look to her for aid, advice, sympathy, and assistance; if the mother allows herself to become the family leaning-post, she may also be repeating the one-sided business of supplying too much force to others and getting none back. She may be practising a false and injurious species of motherhood because it is exacted, begged, or dragged from her. She may be robbing herself of the new life which awaits her, when the brood is reared and their wings are self-sustaining. She is helping the children to make her a feeble, witless, " old woman."

Perhaps one remarks: " If your suggestion was literally followed, the streets would be full of children turned by parents out of their homes and unable to provide for themselves."

So they would. I argue here no literal following of the example set by bird and beast. It would be a great injustice. No custom, when followed for ages, even if based in error, can be suddenly changed without disturbance, injustice, and wrong. Yet it is worth our while to study this principle that we find in nature, from the tree that casts adrift the ripe acorn, to the bird or animal that casts adrift the relatively ripened young. Neither acorn, bird or animal, when cast off or weaned, ever return to the parent for self-sustaining power. Such power, in these cases, is only given by the parent until the new organization is strong enough to absorb and appropriate of the elements about it, absorb of earth and sunshine, or of flesh or grain, the **nourishment necessary to its support.**

Are not our streets today full of grown-up children, quite unable to provide for themselves? Do not thousands leave parental homes with no self-sustaining power, who are all through life unable to feed, clothe, and shelter themselves, save by long hours of drudging labor at the lowest wages? Does not this life of drudgery exhaust and cut them off prematurely? Are there not thousands of daughters all over the land, who will become "old maids," and whose parents will not permit them, were they so disposed, to go out in the world and take their chances? These are the birds cuddled in the nest, until their wings, denied exercise, lose at last all power or prompting for flight, and whose mouths, though they become grown-up birds, are trained only to open and receive the morsels dropped in them.

THE USE OF A ROOM.

Copyright, 1888, by F. J. Needham.

Every person should have a room entirely to him or herself. Great care should be taken regarding those who for social or business purposes are admitted to such room.

It should be a room into which the sunshine may enter as much as possible. It should not be on the north or shady side of the house, for the cold and shady side of any material thing is a reflection in the physical of the shady and forbidding side of the spiritual, and if permanently lived in is certain to cast such reflection on your mind, and is not beneficial to physical health.

A room into which no sunshine can enter cannot be either materially or spiritually purified.

You need one place in the universe to which you can retire when you feel inclined, and shut out everything else so long as you desire; you need one place that you can call wholly your own, not subject to any one's invasion, and not to be entered by any one else without your permission.

You need such a place to rest and gather your forces together. Because when you are a great deal among people, you must absorb more or less of their thought. You will then often see as **the inferior** mind sees. You cannot rid yourself of this thought unless you are at times alone. Your own mind has then opportunity given it to assert its power. As it does, it will throw off the power or thought of other minds, and see for itself.

More than this; when you have a room sacred to yourself, you open the door and grant much more abundant opportunity for wiser and higher intelligences to reach you and give you of their mental richness. They can give you ideas of great use in the practical affairs of life.

You are also placing yourself in the higher and constructive current of thought, all of whose influence is to build you up and make you more and more a power for doing good, first to yourself, next to others.

You are very much out of the reach of these improving agencies if constantly in the world's current of thought; if constantly associated with others who never get out of its hurry, worry, bustle and care. And a single person or companion, if constantly with you, or accessible to you at any hour, can bring you as much of this lower and damaging thought as could ten persons. It matters not whether one person holds the door open to such lower current or one hundred persons.

In this use of a room, I do not mean that one should live a hermit in one; I imply only that temporary withdrawal from others necessary to get ourselves together. There are proper times for seclusion and times for association and society.

If two persons are in sympathy and faith with these

truths, the desire will grow more and more upon them as they see more and more clearly, to give real aid to each other; to help build each other up into more health, happiness and power. One will never object to the other's occasional complete privacy and seclusion, knowing, as they will, the great benefits derived from it, and the certainty that each will share in the other's benefit.

For as you are built up in health, or in any power for drawing to you the best goods of the world, you must, through the sending of the strong desire to similarly benefit the person you most love, give such benefit to that person, providing he or she is in the same faith, belief, or order of thought as yourself.

It is not necessary, while alone in your room, that you try to have your mind strongly set on putting yourself in a higher realm of thought, or drawing higher intelligences to you. You will be most liable to derive benefit from such sources when your hands are occupied with some detail of your toilet, or in the doing of any work not irksome to you.

The mood in which you dress yourself, or perform any so-called trivial act, is the agency, and creates the thought-atmosphere into which beneficial or injurious unseen individuality can enter. If it be the mood of peevishness, despondency or irritability, it taps, so to speak, that current of thought, and on that current of thought, individualized intelligence of the same order can come and annoy you. If the mood in which you brush your hair is one of serenity, repose, and a certain loving absorption in the act itself, you connect yourself with the calmer, clearer, more peaceful, and at the same time more powerful current of thought, and on that the more calm, serene, individualized intelligence or ministering spirit can come to you, full of love, desire and power, to soothe your troubled mind and give you ideas, which in time will grow to forces sufficient to carry you and keep you permanently beyond the action of the disturbed thought-element of the world about you.

No possible effort of body is, in the spiritual sense, trivial. For any act must be done in some mood or condition of mind, and the mood in which you do one thing is the open door to the same mood in the doing of the very next act. If you snatch your hat hurriedly from the peg it hangs on, you are all the more liable to carry that hurried and careless mood into the most important act of your life.

Order and method are the grand factors of success in any business or art. When you practice order and method in your room, you send order and method into your business or art. The tying of a knot in a deliberate, reposeful manner, sends at that moment the element of deliberation, repose and power as a force pushing in your favor, and so acting on other minds far from you. You are so working your force far from your body, when in writing you shape a single letter symmetrically, and not make lines and angles which you expect others to recognize as letters.

Your room all your own, and not liable to invasion from others without your permission, is your workshop, where you can build up those "frames of mind" which you desire permanently to live in. If you cannot assert yourself with others, you can, when so alone, with yourself. The more you do this by yourself the more do you increase your power for doing it with others. You can in your room build up a positive frame of mind, often so necessary for refined and sensitive natures in their contact with the world. You can then go out with this positive frame of mind as with an armor, and are then the less likely to be browbeaten, disconcerted and dominated temporarily by those rough, arrogant natures, whose ruling inward motive it is to make every one else bend to their will. You may not accomplish this at once. You will in time. For every "frame of mind" you so put on, with right and justice as the ruling motive, adds to you an increase of power never to be lost. You may not see your growth in this direction immediately. But you will as the years roll on.

You must be entirely alone at times to build up such states of mind.

As we have said many times before, your thought acts far from your body. It acts on others for or against you. It is always so improving or injuring your business and material interests. It is predjudicing people in your favor or against you, according as you send it out in good will or in the mood of anger. It is necessary to repeat this to ourselves many times. And every reminder, by word or in print, binds this most important truth more and more to us, makes it more and more a part of ourselves, and in this way reminds us more and more to check an unpleasant flow of thought toward another.

It is while your body is isolated in your room that your thought may act the strongest for **beneficial** results to you on others. It is not necessary, providing you are in the right condition of mind, that you try to send it to others. That would be a trying with the physical body so to send it. The right mental condition is that of repose, serenity and good-will. That condition is a force of like character. It is a volume of such force ever going from you. It bears your special purpose or aim along with it to other minds whose motive and purposes are similar, and who, in time, will meet you physically and co-operate with you in the physical realm of life, as their minds are now doing in the realm of thought, which is by far the most powerful for effecting results in the material. Indeed, it is the real and only realm in which results are accomplished. They must first be done in the unseen kingdom of thought before they can take shape and can be seen, touched, felt, used, and enjoyed in the material.

The kind of house you are to live in years hence, the quality of clothing you are to wear, the style of furniture you will use, are being made now in your mind. If you do not aspire to the better house, clothing and furniture; if you say in mind, "I can't have the better," then you are surely putting up the bars against the better. You are then making the inferior and continuing in it.

When any room is devoted to a purpose, or when only a certain character of thought is put out in that room, it is literally filled more and more with such thought. Its power for good or ill continually increases. In other words, your condition of mind fills that room and also goes out from it. Any sensitive person will feel your mental condition immediately on entering. If such mental condition there is permanently peaceful, they will feel that peace. If it is much of the time disturbed, they will soon feel such disturbance.

All rooms are filled with the thought-element most put out by those who live in them, and this element left there acts on people more or less strongly, in proportion to their sensitiveness or capacity to feel the thoughts of others. For such reason you feel the devotional thought of a church, even when empty. You will feel there very different than if in an empty bar-room.

In a room where murder, robbery, or trickery has long been planned, or even thought, if never externally carried out, there is the thought of murder, robbery, or trickery in its air. Such element left there will predispose some to these crimes. If they dare not commit them, it will still cause them to entertain such thoughts, and amuse themselves by living in them. Another class of minds who are above the doing of these wrongs, even in mind, will be made very uncomfortable by this thought left there. Because, such order of mind, though it can not allow such thought to enter or be absorbed, will be occupied much of the time in resisting or throwing off an element foreign to it, and this constant resistance becomes soon exhausting, and causes unpleasant sensations.

A room where only business is thought or talked, soon becomes filled with a business thought-element. It becomes more and more connected with **a business** thought-current. Ideas and plans for conducting business will come to those who so occupy and use that room quicker than in any other place. The more of system and order that pervades such room, the more of system and order will characterize the business. The prevailing mood in that room will be the prevailing mood in the business. If such room is entered or occupied at times by shiftless, reckless, and careless people, they will leave their thought there. This will adulterate and injure the thought-atmosphere of the room. More or less of their thought will be absorbed by the more methodical and better regulated mind, and that carelessness is very liable in some way to be acted out.

The movable tabernacle of the Jews during their exodus from Egypt, contained the apartment known as the "Holy of Holies," into which none but the high priest could enter. It was in such room that the wonderful power was generated which was evidenced in so many miracles during this era of Jewish history. This power was the thought-element of a very few minds bent on a purpose, thought of or talked out in a certain place. Thoughts, especially when talked out in a certain room, are literally left there. The more that such thoughts are so talked out, the more are they left there, and the more of their power is left there, providing it is not mixed up with the thought and talk of other persons different in purpose and motive.

If such thoughts are concentrated on a purpose, say the furtherance of a movement, the growth of a business, the more of the peculiar power necessary to further such movement or business, is left there. You take that power with you when you leave that room and enter on the business or movement. You clothe yourself, on going out, with that thought-element. On meeting with others in any way interested in such business or movement, it acts on them in your favor.

It is an element, also, which attracts to you those interested like yourself, and of like motive. If you think and talk only of trickery in a room, the power you so generate will clothe you with an atmosphere of trickery, attract tricksters to you, and aid you in wrong doing and trickery which may succeed for a time, but is certain, through the operation of an inevitable law, to lead to misery at last.

There is loss of this power coming of talking important business at random, and in any and all places. You leave then more or less of your power in those places. If you talk it truly in a certain room, and with another or others, in earnest like yourself, you are storing up of that power or thought-element in that room, to draw from when you wish.

Any room and all that is in it is literally saturated with the kind of thought most put out and talked in that room. You are placed, so to speak, in a bath of such thought when you enter it. If tattle, back-biting, scandal, and envy is most put out there, you are then in a bath, and absorbing tattle, back-biting, envy and scandal. If peace, gentleness, control of mind and good-will to all is the thought most put out there, you are in a bath of peace, gentleness, control of mind and good-will, and will, in time, **feel their** good effects. If a room is specially devoted to any art, such as painting, sculpture, or music, or to the study and carrying out of any invention, the thought-atmosphere of that room will become more and more highly charged with power to aid, improve, and give new ideas relative to such art, providing that only those enter there who are in a live sympathy with such art and invention, and who have also a live desire to improve themselves and benefit others.

Into such a room, saturated with such thought-element, individualized intelligence, unseen, as regards material bodies, and skilled in the particular art, invention or purpose to which such room is devoted, can come and give in their way great aid in the advancement of such art, invention or purpose.

But if your studio, be it the studio for art or business, invention, or writing, be also a gossiping place, a place free for idle, purposeless minds to enter and while away an hour, a place for low and scurrilous jest, there is brought and left an injurious atmosphere of thought. It is an adulteration of lower thought-element, and will surely retard your advancement in the art, invention, purpose or business.

It leaves an atmosphere into which the higher mind of unseen intelligences cannot readily enter. It is as muddy waters flowing into the crystal stream.

No matter what purpose or what business you are engaged in, that purpose or business will, in accordance with these laws, be greatly aided if you have one room specially devoted to its planning, and talking it over with others interested in it; and if no other kind of thought enters it, the idea-giving atmosphere of such room, devoted solely to such purpose, becomes more and more powerful.

You will find that in a room so used and kept free from injurious thought-elements, your skill in any art will increase more rapidly than elsewhere. If it is your business-room, or "Holy of Holies," plans for pushing business will there be presented more abundantly and more clearly than in any other place.

Always remembering, that where the thought of right, justice, and good-will predominate in any place, there will be generated the greatest power for the art, business or purpose, and the world is to know that the highest art and most successful business must be based on right, justice, and good-will.

The stage of a theatre is a place isolated from the body of the house. In and about that place, the predominant thought put out by many minds is that relative to acting. Such place then becomes filled with that thought. It is for such reason that the actor there feels a greater power and greater ease in throwing himself into his part than he would in a hall or a private house, where other kinds of thought were put out.

The same law prevails regarding the private room of the banker or financier. Such places hold more of their thought and business power than any others.

Your room, so used and filling with the best character of thought, will act as a magnet to attract to you that association most pleasant and profitable to you. It is not natural that man or woman should live alone. It is right that every man and woman should find his or her complement or "completement" in one of the opposite sex — and **only one**.

I do not here imply that these temporary seclusions and uses of a room are *all* that is necessary to increase our power. I do imply that temporary isolations of this nature form an indispensable *part* of the process for so increasing our power.

"How do you know all you state in this matter to be true?" some may ask. I know these ideas are based in truth, partly because I have proved them so far as I have gone. But it is not for me to prove them entirely. It is for you who read these books with that interest which must come with a certain degree of faith, to take hold of these ideas, so far as you feel inclined, and test them for yourselves. To be always a hearer, because it is pleasant to hear, and to do for one's self little or nothing in accordance with the thing heard, will bring little advancement in any direction. Now you will do exactly in proportion to your faith in these things. You will do little or nothing if you have no faith. If you have none, you are not to be blamed.

The White Cross Library is now in the third year of its existence. It was started and has grown in accordance with the business principles it has put forth. We have now readers in every part of the world. We have used none of the old methods for pushing our business. We do not advertise our books. We ask no one to advertise in them. We have had no publishing house to put us before the public. We commenced this publication in an obscure Boston photographic studio, and with barely enough money to print one thousand copies of the first number. We had then not a single subscriber. We knew not where to look for any. We have never sought subscriptions. We have only used means to show the book, and let the results come that were to come.

We used there a room, and only one room, to talk over our business. We talked it only with those specially interested. We have rarely talked it in public places or among crowds, as in restaurants, or any places where people congregate, and if inadvertently we did so at times, felt that we were doing a wrong to ourselves. We have received many hundreds of letters from individuals, commending the principles we put forth, and thanking us for the help we have been the fortunate agency for giving them. We have received many voluntary and favorable criticisms in various newspapers, which have been accorded us unsolicited.

We have seen some dark hours and discouraging periods. They were needless. We made them in our own minds, through uncontrollable fears. We do not assume to practice all we suggest in these books. But the ability so to do grows, and will continue to grow, as it will with you. Knowledge can come in an instant. Growth from such knowledge must take time.

We demand or pray, when in our room, for power to push our business. We demand, also, more faith in that power. We do not pray on our knees. We do not desire in any set form of words. We simply enter on our discussion or presentation to each other of any idea or detail of our business, in that silent attitude of mind or mental condition which trusts and calls for wisdom higher than our own to aid our conferences. We avoid anything like argument.

If there are differences of opinion which cannot be immediately reconciled, we wait a day or two, knowing that the medium course or right way will always in time be presented. We make no rigid rule for the time or form of our conferences, though aiming to have them at a set period.

In this way we hold that we make the real power which is pushing our business ahead. We cannot tell how this power works as regards detail. But we know it does work by the proofs, and we are bent on material results rather than on the immediate solution of mysteries.

We do not call our business a "cause." We solicit no favors or donations for a "cause." We call ours a business. We place a certain value on the ideas we present, as we would on any merchantable commodity. As we receive that value, we are placed above the temptation and error of soliciting donations for doing a good work. We think ours a good work, and think it is all the better for making it sustain and support itself as it goes along. We expect in the success of our business to prove a principle and a law. We say, then, to all others, "So much of this law and this principle as we are here able to present, is as much yours, to use and work on, as it is ours." It is as free as air. We prove it, and by it attain now a certain success, and expect in the future to attain a much greater one. Can we do you a greater favor, than in showing you a law for the attainment of success in any undertaking, which is as much your property to use as ours?

HUSBAND AND WIFE.

COPYRIGHT, 1888, BY F. J. NEEDHAM.

A GREAT mass of men and women live today in spirit and action in separate worlds of their own. These are neither healthy nor natural worlds. The man often lives in his business, art, trade, or profession. He goes to the office, store, workshop, or other place in the morning, is absent all day, and returns at night. In thousands of cases, the woman, the wife, is quite ignorant of this business and its details. She could not take charge of it in case of her husband's sickness. She must leave that to others, and may, therefore, in case the husband loses his body, become at the mercy of others.

Many married women live almost entirely in the world of the household, the care of their children, and, to greater or lesser extent, in shopping, and associating during the day with companions of their own sex.

Many husbands and wives know relatively very little of each other's pursuits. The wife knows that her husband is a lawyer, a merchant, a blacksmith. That is nearly all. The man, in many cases, knows so little of household work, care, and responsibility, as to sometimes imagine, in the vague conception he has of these things, that he "could do it all in an hour," involving the sweeping, dusting, mar-

"Love is Life."

keting, and all other of the manifold efforts required from cellar to garret, from kitchen to closet, to keep a house in good order.

How can you have a live, appreciative sympathy with your wife's household efforts and her world, when you know so little of it? How can you, the wife, have a live, appreciative sympathy in your husband's business, when you know so little about it? When you visit his store, his law office, his workshop, you know little or nothing of the things he uses, or of the character of his efforts. Merchandise, bales, barrels, books, ledgers, metal, wool, cotton, oil, whatever he may deal with, are no more to you, and suggest no more, than when you first saw them. They become in time things dull, unmeaning, and tiresome.

In mind the husband often brings these things and this business home with him. It may be trade, law, speculation, invention, medicine, some art, some science, some profession. He may sit at the table eating, and be absorbed in the thought of these things. His mind may be on them in the evening. He may amuse and entertain you at such times by writing a letter to some business correspondent in Calcutta.

Where is he during these moods? In the room where his body is? No. A person may not be where their body is at all. A person is really where their thought travels. If that thought is for half an hour fixed intently on a person in Calcutta, and the body is in New York, there is far more of the real person acting in Calcutta than in New York.

Your husband brought his body home, but forgot

Sympathy is Force.

to bring his mind with it. His mind was probably in Calcutta when he opened the front door. If his is an agreeable and entertaining mind, when he keeps it where his body is, and allows it to act on that body in talking and expressing ideas to entertain you, you are then deprived of his agreeable company during these temporary sojourns in Calcutta, or possibly at the club, or in the court of law, or some other place where he expects to be next day, and really is now.

During the period of courtship, you may recollect that on coming to see you, he brought oftener his mind and body together, and was not so much temporarily absent in Calcutta as at present. It was then necessary to bring mind and body in the house at once, and keep them both there, because you were not then, possibly, quite won, and therefore it was necessary for him to be lively and entertaining until the winning process was over. It was not then so safe for him to temporarily visit Calcutta as at present.

These temporary visits of your husband to Calcutta would not be so irksome to you could you but go there in spirit with him, and have similar objects of interest whereon to fix your mind. But he goes alone in his own world, and leaves you behind in your world; that is, the best world you can make for yourself, under the circumstances, when you are longing to enter into and blend yourself with your husband's world, and all his worlds and fields of thought.

This is the wife's real place and divine right.

If long experience has not made you callous and indifferent to this domestic life in separate worlds, to this occupancy by two bodies of the same room with only a half union of spirit, you may grieve, or feel a certain disappointment or sense of unrest, coming of, you scarcely know what. You have a "good husband," as the world goes. He provides well for you. You think you ought not to complain; yet you cannot avoid a sentiment of complaint. You ask, "Is this, then, all there is of wedded bliss? Has it, indeed, settled down to a monotone of a house, a home, a husband, all that the world says a woman should expect in marriage — and Calcutta, every evening?

If you have unconsciously become callous, and made up your mind to accept a man's body as congenial company when his mind is somewhere, you may join the ranks of a world of women now existing, whose husbands' minds are almost always in some Calcutta, far or near. There is a world of married women who have formed an exclusive woman's world. They associate with women more than with men. They find in their own sex more companionship. They shop together. Their calls by day are on other married women. The man is absent; necessarily so, it is argued, at his business.

In thousands of places called "homes," the entrance of the husband, or, indeed, of any man, into a room where two or three members of the married woman's world is gathered, is the signal for a cessation of their conversation, or the dispersal of the group. Why? Because, through long usage, either they dare not continue their talk before him, or do not consider that it interests him. It is exclusively of their own world. Nor is it easy for a man to enter

Sympathy is Force.

this world, even if disposed. He will feel a barrier 'twixt him and it. He will feel their reluctance to continue the talk which before his entrance so interested them. He will sometimes feel that for the time they wish him away. And so they do.

He will feel as much out of place as would a lady who should intrude on a group of men "down town," talking stocks, or politics, or business, or so much that passes for business, or intrudes itself into business to enliven it.

For they are then in their peculiar masculine world —a world which men for many ages have been making, and which it is very difficult for a woman to enter.

Up to a certain age, boy and girl associate together in a perfect companionship. They play together, and with equal pleasure, and equal agility also, race, run, jump, climb fences, trees and hay-ricks, coast on the snow in winter, and ramble in wood and field in summer.

Why should not this equality of companionship continue later on? What real gain is there that the young man in his boating, his ball play, and in much of his recreation should live in an exclusive world of his own, into which the girl is admitted more as a looker-on than a participant; although in this participation she is, of late years, gaining ground.

Ages on ages ago, man argued that he was better fitted for many occupations, by reason of superior strength of muscle, than women.

But man did not know that without the **nearness** of the feminine element, or thought, his **strength of**

"Love is Life."

muscle would fail him. He did not know that when a greater closeness of sympathy and combination of interests is formed between man and wife, the greater will be his strength of both mind and muscle. He did not know that it was her strength, also, that did the work. He did know that if he took all her strength, and gave none in sympathy back, that the supply was going all to one side, and that in consequence, both in time would lose all strength.

What is meant by "taking her strength?" This: that when a woman's thought is in any degree of sympathy directed on a man, he receives of that thought-current a literal strength for mind and body.

Why has dancing more exhilaration when the sexes dance together, than when they attempt this exercise separately? Because the combination of the masculine and feminine thought-elements gives to each such exhilaration.

Without nearness of the feminine thought-element, men wear out the sooner physically, as has been proven in the remote mining districts of the West, inhabited exclusively by men.

This exclusive world of women is as unhealthy and unnatural as is the exclusive world of men. In the man's world, woman is an intruder. In the woman's world, man is an intruder. Wherever the masculine element throws out the feminine, there is coarseness. Wherever the feminine element throws out the masculine, there comes narrowness and an excess of prudishness, which may at last reach such an extreme as to see evil in everything masculine. This makes minds really impure.

Sympathy is Force.

Where, in this way, the masculine mind discards and rejects any part of the feminine mind, there comes, as a result, a corresponding amount of mental and physical weakness. Where the feminine mind similarly throws out the masculine, and lives in its exclusive world, there comes to the feminine a similar mental and physical weakness.

"He created them male and female." Nowhere in nature has the Spirit of Infinite Good, or God, made a world exclusively masculine or exclusively feminine. You find this in the forest and the fields; for all through the vegetable kingdom there is the male plant, or principle, and the female plant, or principle; and these two are necessary for the relatively perfect growth or fruition of each other. The strawberry bed, the field of corn, will not thrive unless these two elements are brought together.

In those more complicate expressions of thought, the masculine and feminine minds, or spirit, these spiritual forces acting on each other, produce far greater results. The masculine and feminine thought needs to be blended in all interests, in all business, in all recreation, in all life. Where it is so blended, even though imperfectly, there is more life.

The feminine thought is different in its nature from the masculine. It acts on the masculine nature both as a rest and a stimulant, or inspiration. It gives to the man an actual strength to use in his trade or business, which, often in his ignorance, he supposes to be entirely his own, and drawn altogether from himself. Your husband may not be able to write and go in spirit to Calcutta, unless **you**, his

"Love is Life."

wife, are in the room, or at least in the house. If you are not there, he feels uneasy. He cannot "fix his mind" on anything. When you come in, and are seated, he can go on with his work, and amuse you with his pen scratching.

Why is this? Because the feminine element, your thought, which he absorbs from you, is giving him the very strength he uses to go to Calcutta. He feels something, he can't tell exactly what, that gives him a sensation of ease and comfort when you are near. That is caused by your thought of love and sympathy flowing toward him. He feeds on that as much as on bread.

If your thought and sympathy was turned entirely on another man, or entirely on other interests, he would feel restless and uneasy, though entirely ignorant that your affections had strayed in another direction.

Some husbands cannot entertain their wives by silently poring over their newspaper or book for hours, unless the wife is in the room. The actual strength to read the paper comes from the force absorbed of the woman's thought.

In like manner, the husband uses his wife's strength in business at the store, the office, the workshop,— everywhere. For love and sympathy sent any one, is a source of strength as much as is bread or meat.

Why, at middle age, does the man so often lose his body after the death of the material part of his wife? Because he is cut off from this supply of the feminine element, which he has absorbed, and used, and been nourished by, all his life.

Sympathy is Force.

Whose fault is this? Is it entirely that of the man? No. It rests as much with the woman as with the man. It rests with neither, so long as they are in complete ignorance of their use and value to each other. If you are daily the recipient of something that keeps you alive, and know not that you do receive it, or that such a substance exists, or that it keeps you alive, you cannot be censured for acting and living in a different manner from what you would, or should, did you know these things.

But when you are thoroughly awakened to the fact that you are giving of your very life to another, that it is you who supply an element to that other, which may keep him alive, and keep him in a condition to do business, if then you make no demand to receive from that other an equivalent in return, then it is you who are at fault.

What is this equivalent you should receive? That of the flow of your husband's thought to you in the desire to entertain you during your mutual hours of leisure, as his thought so went out to you before marriage, when he wished to woo you. Such thought would cheer and strengthen you in mind and body, even as it once did. Food, clothes, and a shelter, are not all your necessary vital supplies. You are not supposed to have married for these. You married your husband's mind. You were attracted by that mind. You liked it. You received from it during courtship an element which was a source of pleasure. You do not receive so much now, and feel a loss. It is because he is, when by your side, too **much in Calcutta.**

"Love is Life."

He has the right to use the force he absorbs from you in the day's business. He has no right to come home at night, draw it still from you, and use it in more business. He should use it in mind, as he did when he was glad to walk, possibly miles, through snow or rain, to chat an hour with you.

If he and you together think it a necessity so to use this force constantly, at any and all times of day and night, in any one special pursuit or business, then you are not aware that for purpose of your mutual recreation and recuperation, these, your mutual forces, should be used in varied pursuits, so that one department of mind should rest while another is employed. Business is not as well done when a man's mind runs on business day and night, at meal times, and all hours. Such habit breaks men down prematurely, and is one road to insomnia and insanity. When we feel, as we may, at times, that we are "tired of everything," and the world and all in it seems worn out for us, it is because one department of mind and life is overtaxed. We lack, then, the ability or knowledge of getting into another side of life and living in that. True man and wife will know in time many sides of life, so to get into and live, which may now be neglected altogether.

The feminine mind and organization receives first all finer and higher thought or idea. It transmits this thought or force to the masculine mind to which it is most attracted. The feminine mind and organization is the finer and more delicate instrument for so receiving and transmitting such idea. The masculine thought and element is vitally necessary to

Sympathy is Force.

keep this instrument in the best repair, to give it strength, cheer, and support, through love.

The masculine mind is as the trunk and root supporting branch and leaf. Trunk and root are more of the earth, and are harder and stronger. Yet if the leaves are destroyed, trunk and root will die. The feminine mind is as the branches and leaves of the tree, which first catch the sunlight, as the feminine mind first catches the higher and finer thought and force. So if anything prevents the feminine mind from performing its proper office, that of receiving the finer impression, the masculine mind will suffer, and the masculine body suffer, also, in sympathy. The feminine mind, or spirit, will droop and wither, unless it receives this strength of the masculine thought. If the mind droops, so in time will the body.

The masculine mind will be far more clear, vigorous, and evenly balanced, when it learns, as it will, in time, to respond always to this flow of thought from the feminine, and not as it receives this strength from the feminine, to expend it always on efforts other than those of being a real companion to the wife. When man and wife are together, their minds should be together. Their minds are not together when one is doing something that the other can take no interest in. Their minds are not together when one-half the husband's mind is constantly on interests in which, for the wife, there is no live, acting partnership.

This "partnership" means something more than the mere telling by husband and wife of each other's

---
"Love is Life."

troubles. Nor is it a growling to each other, in confidence, of their respective troubles. What good results from telling your perplexity to a person who has no power to assist you, and in whose judgment you have little or no confidence?

This interchange and blending of the masculine and feminine thought is an absolute necessity to health and vigor to body and mind of each. When this law is more understood and practised, men and women in the married state will attain to higher and healthier conditions of body than can now be realized. Because, in so giving and receiving of their respective kinds of thought, there comes a fruition attainable in no other way. By "fruition," we mean strong, elastic, supple muscles; increasing ability to enjoy all things; and, in place of decay, a constant building up of their respective spirits; and what builds up their spirits, must also build up their bodies.

The decay and weakness of body called "old age," is a state of the body coming of the misuse or misdirection of the masculine and feminine spiritual or thought-forces. Those forces can be as powerful to build bodies up, and reform them ever with newer and newer material, as they are now powerful to take them to pieces.

The two worlds in which so many men and women, husbands and wives, now live, bring, through the separation of these forces, disease, decay, and death. Their lack of blending in each other's interests and occupations is certain, in time, to bring a lack of love. Now love is not endurance. Love is not a feeling on the wife's part that she ought to be content, or will

Sympathy is Force.

try to be content, when if she put the question closely enough to herself, she would be obliged to own to herself that she felt the lack of her husband's attentions — the attentions of courtship; and more — for a true love will increase, in its desire to please, rather than lessen.

Love is literally life. The lack of it leads to death.

This unnatural world, in which so many women now dwell, is the greatest aid in making them harsh and repulsive. It robs them of their attractiveness to the other sex. It causes them, in time, not to care to be attractive. It makes them neglectful of their dress and personal appearance. It takes from life its mainspring for living. It tends to make them narrow, petty, censorious, and gloomy.

Because, be their intent as good as it may, women cannot, in associating for any purpose exclusively with women, get that force spring and impetus which comes from the masculine thought-element.

On the other hand, the unnatural, one-sided, exclusive, man's world, of business, interest, and recreation, deprives him of a vital supply in the element of feminine thought; and this is one and the principal reason why he so often "lets down," a few years after marriage, neglects his attire, becomes a plodder, refuses to entertain new ideas and aims, wants to live in a rut, and becomes, at the age of fifty, an "old man."

As to interest and knowledge, no part of the husband's life can be safely left out of the wife's liveliest sympathy. A loving woman can, and will, learn anything she sets her mind upon.

"Love is Life."

As to interest and knowledge, no part of the wife's life and occupation can be safely left out of the husband's liveliest and loving sympathy.

This is not "sentiment," as that word is sometimes interpreted. It is a law of nature, and its working is universal, from the mineral to man and womankind; for the cruder elements of sex exist in all minerals.

There can be no whole nor happy life without a complete marriage. There is for every man and woman a complement, or completeness, in the opposite sex somewhere. There is but one such complement, or completeness, for every man and woman, through all eternity.

Many a couple, truly married through the law of attraction and Infinite Good, live together in these two worlds today. They live unhappily together. They live unhappily, because they do not know that permanent and increasing wedded happiness comes of the observance of certain laws and mental conditions toward each other. They must, to attain such happiness, become, in all things and interests, of one mind and spirit. If they cannot so become, then they are "yoked unequally together," and are not true man and wife. But they may be "yoked unequally together," temporarily, and certain errors being removed from the minds of one or both, find themselves truly married. More than one couple have found, despite repeated bickerings, and even where, disregarding the usages of conventionality, they have separated, that they cannot avoid coming together again. They do find something in each

Sympathy is Force.

other they cannot find elsewhere. These are truly married, but one or both is immature. But married they are, by the law of God, or Infinite Good, and whom God hath so married, no other man can either truly marry or put asunder.

Many a couple so married, yet not realizing in marriage today, the happiness they expected, nor the happiness they had during courtship, could commence for each other their paradise for eternity, by commencing where some leave off, even at the altar, — commencing the period of courtship over again; commencing the renewal of the little civilities and attentions which characterized that period; the desire to please each other's eyes in care, taste, and neatness of attire; the control of temper and demeanor in each other's presence; the checking of the cutting retort or sarcasm, — commencing to restore those certain barriers and formalities of etiquette which it is never safe for man and wife to disregard and trample over. For, when you allow these barriers to be destroyed, you destroy respect for your personality, and when ever so little of respect is gone, just so much of contempt replaces it; and when the husband bounces into the wife's room, or presence, bringing all his ill humor with him, and with no more sign of respect for what should be the sacredness of such place or presence than he has for his stable, then be sure more or less of his respect for you is lacking.

In this regard the wife, also, may trample down these barriers, as well as the husband.

Commence, also, to ask each other if **what they do**

"Love is Life,"

is pleasing to the other. Commence in pursuits mutually enjoyed, this much-needed blending of minds and flow of their very vitality and force of thought, each to the other, so that it shall build them up in mind and body, and when properly directed, in fortune, also. Let them cease this ruinous separation in spirit, coming of the husband's frequent journeyings in mind, even in his wife's company, to some one or other of his Calcuttas.

It may not, in every case, be easy for such couples to rebuild immediately the edifice of early love thus torn, mutilated and desecrated, through years of neglect. "Use doth breed a habit in a man," and woman, also; and the cross word, the surly demeanor, the outburst of peevishness, may sometimes come, despite all effort at first to prevent it. But enough can be soon done to prove that love can again be placed on its first and right basis; and it can also be proved, that such love between them, and all the pleasure it brings, can be increased, and keep on ever increasing.

And when both have done their best to overcome their infirmities and defects, which have grated and rasped the other, there is a great, Supreme Power, to call upon in mind, and from which we *must* demand that which will make us whole.

Sympathy is Force.

A Cure for Alcoholic Intemperance through the Law of Demand.

COPYRIGHT, 1889, BY F. J. NEEDHAM.

IF men can be cured or rid of an appetite for liquor, there would then be less and less demand for liquor. If people cease to have an appetite for any article kept for sale, there soon will be little or no sale for such article.

We hold that the appetite for liquor can be controlled, through the exercise of a certain mental law. This law is within the reach of all. It can be experimented on without cost. It can be used by the sufferer from this diseased appetite; and be used, at the same time, by his friends in his behalf.

Such friends can use the law of silent demand. That is the power which one mind possesses of silently throwing its thought, or desire, or wish, or expectation, into another mind, and making such mind wish, desire, think, and act, in accordance with the other's wish. This power can be used by one or many minds thinking or desiring in unison. It can be used for good or evil results. It is constantly used all about us, though for the most part unconsciously, with good or evil results.

For instance, the man who drinks will crave liquor the more if much in the society of those who drink. He will feel the craving less if much in the society of the temperate and self-controlled. No word nor argument, for or against the use of liquor, need be made, in these cases, to increase or lessen such craving. It comes of the silent action of mind upon mind.

But this force of silent demand can be used more intelligently, and with quicker profitable result.

If, in your own mind, you will say in thought that you do not expect a friend afflicted with this habit to give way to it, he will, through the force of your mind acting on his own, be strengthened to resist the temptation. If you will, in mind, always positively see him as temperate and self-governed, he will receive from you the force, in thought, of temperance and self-government. If several unite in so sending him this thought, and so seeing him in thought, they give him a proportionately stronger force to resist the uncontrollable appetite. They are, then, really praying for him, and praying in the strongest way. A man is cured of the craving for liquor when he can pass the liquor saloon, or even enter it, without any desire to drink, or can have liquor freely offered him, with no desire to partake of it. He is thoroughly cured when he can take a glass of wine, or other stimulant, without giving way to the inordinate appetite for more.

The bar-keeper is, in many cases, the most thoroughly self-controlled man in the saloon. He may be always in the midst of liquor selling and drinking, but has no tendency to indulge to excess. No intemperate bar-keeper can retain his position. His employer expects him to be temperate. The action of the employer's mind on the employé is one powerful agency in keeping him temperate. The employé feels the employer's thought. He has that part of the employer's mind which expects, and demands, that he shall keep sober, thrown into his own mind, and acts in accordance with such mind.

This is precisely the mental attitude which we should assume toward the victim of excess. We should image him in our minds as temperate, and able to control his appetite. In so doing we send him (our thought being kind, sympathetic, and free from anger or impatience) a force or current of thought, which will cause him to demand of himself to be temperate. If we send him the thought of controlling his appetite, we help him to control his appetite. The more of us who so unite in sending such order of thought to any single individual, the stronger the power brought to bear on that individual to stop his excessive craving for stimulant. It becomes then a co-operative prayer for such individual.

But if we in our minds always see or image that man as a drunkard, we are sending him a current of thought which will aid the more to make and keep him intemperate. We are helping him only to keep before him the image of himself as a drunkard; and if we regard him in spirit as worthless, **depraved,**

Our Thoughts are Forces.

and irreclaimable, we are helping him only to see himself as worthless, depraved, and irreclaimable. We must not in our minds say, "I wish he would control himself," and almost in the same thought say, "I expect or I am afraid he will get drunk the next chance he gets." In so doing, we increase those chances. Nor should we in our minds, when he is absent or present, scold him in anger or impatience for his infirmity. For in such mood of scolding, we shall always see him in mind as the drunkard or the person who irritates, vexes, or grieves us by his inability to control his appetite. We help to cure that inability when, in our minds, we make him a man temperate or self-controlled. We send the force of such a reality in thought to the weak will, so oft overcome by the inordinate craving. We send, on the contrary, the force of the intemperate reality when we image such in our minds, to the same weak will, and increase its burthen.

But it may be asked, "Is not the man a drunkard? Where is the consistency of saying a man is temperate, when he is not, or of seeing him in our minds as temperate, when he is not?"

The real man in this case is *not* a drunkard. The real man is what that man is in his highest aspiration or desire, and it matters not how low or degraded is the material condition of any human being, there remains still in that individual the desire to be something better, or the desire to rid himself of an appetite or habit which brings him pain. The real is the spiritual man or woman. In him or her there is always the spark of aspiration; or, in other words, the desire for improvement, although it may be very feebly expressed. When we send, even to the man in the gutter, this sentiment in thought, "You are not a drunkard. You are not irreclaimable. You are temperate," we are sending to the real man thoughts or forces which feed his spirit and make it stronger.

It is only the material man, or the material part or mind of that man, that is in the gutter. With him in our thought, we have nothing to do. We refuse in mind to see him. We see only in mind that man out of the gutter, erect, clothed, self-controlled, and in his right and higher mind. When so we see him, we are sending him that kind of thought. We are presenting to him, as we so send him such thought, the image or ideal of himself as a true man. But if we see him in imagination always as a drunkard, we help to keep him in mind before himself as a drunkard, and this helps to keep him a drunkard. If we see him in imagination as an inordinate lover of strong drink, it is an aid to keep him before himself as an inordinate lover of strong drink.

The desire of one or many persons to rid another person of an injurious appetite, is the greatest of all power for so ridding him of such appetite, or any other defect. It is a co-operative prayer.

But such desire or prayer, or the law of demand, must, like any other force in nature, be directed aright, or it may do harm instead of good.

If we express this thought in our prayer, "we ask for the reform of this man cursed with an inordinate appetite," or "we ask for the reform of this incorrigible thief," we have still too much in mind the image and thought of an uncontrollable appetite, or an incorrigible thief, and we shall then send this thought to the victim of appetite, or to the thief. That thought acts on them. It does not lift them up. It keeps, rather, excess and thieving ever present in their minds. For the thought that others think of you they send you; and one is very apt to hold himself or herself in his or her own estimation as others esteem them. If one hundred people unite, unjustly, in thinking of you as a thief, or hold you in any other evil estimation, you will have a powerful unseen force acting on you, to make you feel that you are the very character they think you. You may not know where such impression comes from, or that such cause for disposing you to evil exists. But it does exist, and people do others a great deal of temporary harm by so thinking unfavorably of them.

Just as we see a person in mind do we pray for them, or desire them to be. If you will persist ever in seeing a person's present faults, with all the irritation those faults may cause you, you are actually praying or demanding that such person shall remain with such faults. You are sending that person, from time to time, the same faulty, defective portions of himself, in instalments, to add to himself. You may even have a certain pleasure in talking that person over and over, and raking up all his or her shortcomings, and the annoyances they have caused you. You are then doing that person much harm, and harm in proportion as your love for raking up the old annoyances increases.

Our Thoughts are Forces.

When people are always scolding about the faults of another, they really beget in themselves a love for such scolding. They beget in themselves a morbid and unhealthy love of fault-finding. If the person with whom they find fault was suddenly made relatively perfect, their occupation would be gone. They would feel uneasy, because they could no longer image him in their minds as the "poor, miserable creature" he had been.

No thought cuts deeper to the heart of an intemperate person than the feeling, on his part, that his friends do not, in their minds, trust him in the use of liquor. The feeling that the bottle is put out of sight, because he has entered the room, has made many a man rush from that room or place, and rush into excess. Why is this? Because a force or thought has been sent him, and has entered into him, and became a part of him, for the time, telling him that he is weak, untrustworthy, and relatively worthless. If he is placed on the same footing of indulgence as the others, and if the others say to him in their minds, "We expect and know that you will govern your appetite as we do," they will give him a mental help to govern that appetite, because a stronger, more encouraging, and aspiring order of thought has been sent him from those persons, and has entered into and acts on him.

If three, five, or ten persons are in a room, and they will, by previous agreement, make up their minds that the next person who enters that room shall be made to feel a certain emotion, or be put in a certain mood of mind, they will be very likely to throw such

Our Thoughts are Forces.

mood on that person, provided their minds and attention or concentration of thought is not taken off such person by the entrance of others, or by other causes of interruption. They may, by this method, make that person feel awkward, or constrained, or very cheerful, in accordance with the character of thought they unite in thinking of him for the time. As they for the time image that person in their minds, so will they, to greater or less extent, make that person feel. What they may imagine, in concert, that person to feel and act for the time being, are they desiring or praying for that person to be. Prayer is the putting out of a strong desire or demand. It can be so put out for a good or ill purpose. We can pray for evil as well as good, and many do, unconsciously, pray for evil rather than good. If I, as a bigot, see another person always as a miserable, fallen creature, full of faults, and also desire that such person shall feel very uncomfortable, shall be harassed and disturbed in mind, shall live in a gloomy and despairing state of mind, until such person accepts my opinions and is converted to them, I am doing the wrong thing, and using prayer, or the law of demand, in the wrong direction; because I am then both judging and punishing, through the power of thought. I have no right so to inflict pain on others. That is man's erroneous method. It is not the method of God, or the Spirit of Infinite Good. That method is to convert and change men's natures through pouring on them sunshine, and not darkness. That method is to make them feel cheerful, joyful, and uplifted into temperance and self-control, as I so image them in my mind, and send such image in thought to them. When I do this, I connect myself with the Spirit of Infinite Good; I feel better myself than if I in mind scold or threaten, or see ever the degraded being or uncontrollable appetite.

At present too many of us are so seeing the sufferer through alcoholic intemperance. As so these many minds see him are they praying for him in the wrong direction. They are co-operatively handling this gigantic unseen power of thought to keep the drunkard and the criminal down, by always seeing him as a drunkard or criminal, and never forgetting that he has been one. They are unable to forget it. They are very liable to show before such person that they are not able to forget it. If they cannot forget, they must make that person feel it. Because thought, as a force, travels from mind to mind, and acts from mind to mind; and if in your mind you cannot forget that the person before you has been a criminal or a drunkard, you are certain to make that person feel your unspoken opinion of him.

A man should never be spoken or thought of as a "reformed drunkard." To help keep him self-controlled, we need to forget that he has ever been a drunkard. We have nothing whatever in our minds to do with him as a drunkard. We need to bury the former drunkard, bury him so deep in forgetfulness that he can never be dug up again. If we do not, if in thought we keep up a fear he may relapse into his former habit; if we are ever admonishing him to keep sober; if we carry that thought with us when in his company, or out of it, we may be **more**

Our Thoughts are Forces.

to blame than he if he does fall; for we have, in such case, been sending him, in thought, the image and force of his fallen self, instead of the image and force of a strong man able to control his appetite.

If on a very dark night you walk the street, and some one falsely calls out, "Look out! There's a hole just ahead of you!" you will for a moment think, feel, and walk as if there was a hole ahead of you. You will, in imagination, see yourself tumbling into it. A power of thought has been thrown on you by another to make you so feel.

The temperance lecturer sometimes talks drunkenness a whole evening. The mental pictures given the audience are sometimes those of his old self in the gutter. He may dig up his old degraded self and exhibit it. Sometimes he excites laughter through humorous representations of degradation. Sometimes he scolds, threatens, and even abuses those engaged in the liquor traffic.

Is this a healthy order of thought to throw on an audience?

"But people must be warned against the evil of liquor drinking," you may say. True. But sometimes "warnings" run into long-drawn histories of vice, crime, degradation, and create a morbid and unhealthy appetite for more of the same pictures. The long and elaborate account of the execution, the description of the gallows, the close detail of the criminal's demeanor as the hangman's knot is passed over his neck — all this is not a warning, even if the condemned slew his victim in a fit of drunkenness. It is an unhealthy story, which sometimes, after being read by the small boy, induces him to hang and torture the cat, in the spirit of imitation.

If you desired to cure a man of a murderous tendency, would you put him in a place or in surroundings where his thought would be led towards, or away, from murder? Would you call his place of sojourn "The Murderer's Home?" Is a man made the less an inebriate from knowing that he is in an "Inebriate's Home?" or an institution called by any name to remind him continually of an old fault and an old self, which he needs to bury and forget?

When either in words or in thoughts (and thoughts have tongues as well as words) you remind the victim of any defect of character of his old faulty self, and the hole he has so many times tumbled into, you are actually digging for him the hole again, and setting in motion a force to push him into it. You want to cover that hole up, and the drunkard with it, and forget all about it, just as you want the holes you may have fallen into in time past similarly covered up, and your old faulty self covered up and forgotten with it.

We have in our minds nothing to do with the drunkard of yesterday. Bury him. Forget him. In our thought he is today a temperate, self-controlled man. In our mind we expect and demand him so to be. In his own mind he must also hold himself as temperate and self-controlled. We are then praying, and he is praying with us in concert, and in the right way.

But when, after his excess, he goes among people and meets the peculiar look, and *feels* the peculiar thought, which, if put in words, would say, "You have been on another spree; you have disgraced yourself again," then he has in himself, and outside of himself, almost everything to discourage and little to encourage. He sees himself imaged everywhere as a fallen creature. It is then the drunkard being ever dug up. The temperate man is buried.

And by whom? By people who may be faulty as well as he. By people who may pride themselves on being temperate as regards the use of liquor, who may be themselves very intemperate as regards control of temper or mood, or some other physical appetite; who know and can realize nothing of the terrible craving or incessant gnawing, coming, not only of a morbid appetite for stimulant, but from a body ignorantly and unconsciously exhausted in some way of its vitality; a demand and craving which they may be indirectly fostering and feeding, through the injurious thought they may send him. For he needs the image and force in thought of strength and self-control, to send him not the image of weakness and degradation.

Our thoughts of each other do strengthen or weaken each other, do encourage or depress each other.

If the family at the breakfast-table are each in thought saying of the son, whose weakness lies in liquor, "I expect he'll get to drinking again today; I fear he'll go to tippling again with his companions," they are making him feel depressed, weak, untrustworthy, and, consequently, all the more liable to resort to drink for sake of a temporary stimulation. They should say in thought, "He is not going into any excess. He can govern himself. He will govern himself."

The strongest prayer is not the prayer of petition, or supplication, or entreaty. It is the prayer of imperious demand. The Christ of Judea said, "Knock and it shall be opened unto you." When you knock at a door you do not, so far as that knock is concerned, make it in the spirit of begging. You use your force of muscle so that it shall be heard within. If you knock hesitatingly or entreatingly, you will not put so much force in it, and it is not so liable to be heard.

Imperious demand is the heart and essence of prayer. "Be thou healed!" were the words of the Christ of Judea. "I say unto thee, arise!" was his imperious demand to the so-called dead man. "Every sentence of the Lord's Prayer is an imperious demand. What can be more authoritative than "Give us this day our daily bread!" Does it read or mean, "We, thine unworthy creatures, if it please thee, do hope, and beg, and supplicate this day to give us our daily bread?" No. Those terms have, since Christ's time, been added and used by man.

The Spirit of Infinite Good desires that we knock at its door in a similar positive, imperious, demanding mood for whatever we want. It desires to give us of its strongest force ; and to attract this, we must come in our strongest force. We do not come with our strongest force when we say, in words or in thought, "We hope, or beg, or entreat, or supplicate that our friend's uncontrollable appetite **be removed.**"

That is half-way effort. We want to say, "His appetite must be cured. He is cured. He has no uncontrolled appetite. We see him in mind only as a self-governed man. We demand of the Supreme Power that he be made so. We demand that he be made one with God, or the Supreme Power; that he realize himself as a part of that Power; and that, as this Power is wise, temperate, serene, and self-controlled, he must also draw to himself more and more of the same attributes and qualities of Deity."

When all the churches in this land set apart certain days for the exercise of this imperious demand, or prayer, in behalf of the victim of excess; when they so co-operatively unite in seeing and making men whole; when they bury all drunkards and tipplers, and see only these men spiritually as self-controlled, "clothed and in their right minds;" when they cease altogether the prayer of threat or menace, or the desire of inflicting punishment on any one; when this great and positive demand is made in the spirit of love and good will to all, and desire that all men's hearts shall be softened, and inclined more and more to the right way, through the warmth of sunshine, rather than the shadows of a frown, there will come, within a relatively short time, a great change for the better in this respect. Men will leave off their drinking habits, and scarcely know why. A current and force that now sweeps them into the saloon will lose its power. Another mind and spirit will take possession of them. They will gradually be led to realize a better, more permanent, and more healthy stimulation, whose cause and source lies beyond the domain of material science or material things.

If yours is the uncontrollable appetite for liquor, say in your mind not only, "I will conquer this appetite," but "I have conquered it. It is conquered." Then you join your spiritual force with those who regard you in spirit as self-controlled. Your real self or spirit has taken a strong, positive, decided hold in this matter. The material, the body *must* follow in time. But when your spirit was saying, "It's no use, I can't conquer this appetite. It will ruin me in time," the material part of you was "led of the spirit" in the wrong direction. Seeing yourself thus in mind as weak and degraded, is a force to make you so. Whatever you image yourself in mind, you must make of yourself in time. Your image of yourself as temperate, and self-controlled, and your saying that you are so, is the first step in the right direction. You may afterward fail at times. The material appetite may at times get the best of the spirit's aspiration. Yet every time you so fail, you are taking a stronger hold to control yourself, providing in mind you always say, "I have conquered. I am determined to conquer." The periods between your relapses will grow longer and longer. You will find the appetite gradually decreasing. The cure will be gradual, but sure. All permanent cures must be gradual. When you have no longing for liquor, you are cured. When you cease to think of it, your cure is sure and permanent.

If you use liquor, make up your mind before you swallow it, that you will not indulge to **excess, and** that you will not allow what you do take to make you drunk or lose your head. This also is a prayer, a demand, a force working for you in the right direction. The effect of liquor on different individuals is due entirely to their mental conditions. A man who makes up his mind beforehand not to become intoxicated, will keep his head, while if he drinks without a thought of self-control, he will the more quickly lose it.

Our Thoughts are Forces.

THE MYSTERY OF SLEEP, OR OUR DOUBLE EXISTENCE.

(COPYRIGHT BY F. J. NEEDHAM, 1889.

We live, move, act, enjoy or suffer as much during the state called sleep as when awake. We live then through and by those finer spiritual senses possessed by all of us in embryo, and of which the sight, hearing, touch and taste of the physical body are rougher correspondences.

But this portion of our lives is a blank to us when the physical senses resume their sway on awakening, because the physical memory is not capable of receiving and holding but the merest fragments of the scenes, events and occurrences of our lives while the body is unconscious. Such fragments, often incoherent, inconsistent and jumbled, we call dreams.

Our dreams are the dim tracings of a real life—the life realized through these other senses dimly and fragmentarily marked on the physical memory, or memory of what is realized through the physical senses.

In sleep, a chord of thought (the silver link) connects body and spirit, though the spirit may then go far from the body. By that chord your spirit, while your body sleeps, sends that body a current of life of good or evil quality according to the world of thought you live in.

The death or loss of the body comes when this chord is broken. When the mind grows into that condition that it is always receiving of new ideas and truth, that chord becomes stronger and stronger and cannot be broken. We shall then become "as wells of water springing into everlasting life."

We live then two lives quite distinct and separate from each other. The remembrance of each is blotted from the other. The spirit's life during sleep is quite forgotten when awake. On the other hand, our every day's life and existence is unknown to our every night's sleep existence. We are in substance two individuals every twenty-four hours, one having but the vaguest knowledge or acquaintance with the other. We live daily in two worlds close together as regards space, but widely separated by the gulf of unconsciousness.

We have a material memory which will not write down our spiritual existence. We have also a spiritual memory which will not write down our physical or day's existence. One of our lives is a life in physical things with the physical body. The other is a life of spiritual things with the spiritual body and senses.

For as Paul says: "There is a natural body and there is a spiritual body."

This spiritual body exists at the same time as the physical body. It exists also after the loss of the physical body. It existed before the birth of our present physical body.

You are by day and night, sleeping and waking, as two persons who are strangers to each other, yet each having the same spirit. You are as one person having two distinct lives, and two distinct sets of senses for each of those lives. Your spirit by day uses its body as a person who puts on a rough garment to go down in a mine. It does not use this body in the other existence, and yet it thinks it does, for in that existence the spiritual being, through ignorance, thinks itself a physical being, and therefore judges and reasons entirely from its physical senses. But in the higher development of our beings we shall also judge and reason through the finer and far more powerful spiritual senses, whose action is very different and has far greater range than the inferior senses confined to the limitations of the physical body.

Columbus discovered a new physical world. But within and of every one of us there lies half a world, half a life, half an existence, first to be discovered, next cultivated, improved and literally brought out of darkness.

As our minds or spirits grow in this or some other physical existence, these two worlds or existences for each and all of us are to be united so that we shall live in and be conscious of both.

Demand or prayer is certain to bring more knowledge to us of life's mysteries, and knowledge will give our spirits more power. "Prayer without ceasing" (that is, a persistent desire to know the truth) will show by degrees these great powers lying in us in embryo, and what a different thing is life from what we hold it at present.

Then we shall be conscious of both lives and also happily conscious. But such consciousness at present would result in little or no happiness, because the tendency now is, through ignorance, to stray into a world during sleep similar in care, worry, anger and uncontrolled mind, as so many live in during physical consciousness. Happily for us we bring back to the waking or physical memory little remembrance of it. If we did, life might be doubled in misery.

But we do often bring back to the physical world the injurious results of our straying into a lower spiritual world during sleep. Two hours of sleep when your spirit goes to the purer domain of spiritual life will refresh the body far more than ten hours passed in the lower.

Sleep is a condition of unconscious rest and recuperation for the physical senses, but not for our other, the spiritual senses and being. The eye that sees in dreams is not the physical but the spiritual eye—an eye which can see as far as a thought can go; an eye, so to speak, at the end of a thought. The ear which hears in dreams is the spiritual ear; an ear whose power is not confined to a certain limited space.

The physical senses of touch, taste, sight and hearing can only maintain their highest vigor for say ten or twelve hours out of the twenty-four. Keep the body awake for two or three days and all physical sense becomes impaired and blunted.

Our physical senses during the condition called sleep are fed and recuperated from that world or realm of spirit to which we may belong. Our minds or spirits during sleep go into and live in our respective worlds of spirit.

From such realms they gather and return to the body with the quality of that world's thought or element. Such thought may give the body strength or weakness, health or disease. In proportion as our minds are elevated and pure, full of desire to do right and justice, of desire for more and more power to do good to ourselves and all others; of desire for more and more faith in the grand possibilities of existence; faith, also, in the possibility of a physical life, not only free from pain and disease, but one increasing ever in strength, vigor and rejuvenation, will the spirit bring to its body more and more of vigor, health and rejuvenation.

But if the mind is low and narrow, full of jealous and envious thought, believing only in the material world its body sees and feels, and therefore believing that its whole being must decay and die, then such a spirit brings back from its peculiar world during its body's sleep only the elements of decay, death and weakness.

Sleep is not always rest. The disturbed, anxious,

fretting or angry mind on the body's losing its consciousness goes (if no prayer or demand for peace and power intervene) to a realm of disturbance. It brings to the body on waking the element of disturbance. Hence, during the waking hours, disturbance and anxiety predominate.

Similarly, the mind dwelling on disease, goes in sleep to the lower realm of disease. It brings only the thought and element of disease to the body.

Let your mind, then, before going to sleep, be on the thought of health. If the body is in any way ailing, say in thought: "It is only the instrument I use that is ailing. What I think, I am. My spirit and spiritual body is well. Therefore it must during sleep send this physical body health."

Say this to yourself every night, and if immediate relief does not come, remember that you may have a lifetime of error in thought to contend with; that your growth out of this must be gradual, and that the good results from such growth, though gradual, must be sure and lasting.

Our unknown life during sleep is of more importance than our known waking physical life. For it is the life of the spirit, and of the spiritual senses so far as they are developed.

Your real self is not your body, but that invisible force whose only evidence is your daily, hourly thought. Your body is relatively but a thing of yesterday. Your thoughts are your body's foundation. What you think is as the spring which feeds your well of life.

Your spirit feeds your body during sleep with its peculiar beliefs or opinions. If you believe firmly and without a doubt or question that your body must in time weaken, decay and show all the signs of old age, your spirit will surely bring the body the thought elements of weakness and decay. If you will in your waking hours even but entertain the idea that the decay of the body after a certain time of the physical life is *not* an absolute necessity— that because this decay always has been (so far as you are aware), is no proof that it always must be for the race—that a demand on retiring for increase of health, of increasing vigor of mind and body will bring in time such results to you—that a demand or prayer for faith to believe this will in time bring proofs to increase such faith, then such order of thought as persisted in will gradually turn your spirit during the body's unconsciousness from groping about in that lower spiritual realm of positive belief in decay, weakness, disease and death where our race is now wandering. Such thought will gradually turn your mind into the spiritual realm of strength, vigor and youth eternal, and the spirit's effect on the body will in time be not a transient but a permanent good—one which comes to stay.

Your body is always changing its physical elements. It is not the same body you had ten, twenty, thirty or more years ago. Because yours is not the same mind you had ten, twenty, thirty or more years ago. As your mind changes, so your **body** changes. As you grow continually into new **truths,** new elements from the spiritual will come to renew the body.

Your belief, be it what it may, materializes itself in your body. Believe implicitly in the absolute necessity of disease and decay, and your blood and flesh will become a material expression of disease and decay. Do but entertain the idea that disease and decay are not absolute necessities, and in a relatively little time your flesh and blood will have changed to an extent for the better, and as your belief grows (as it must) it will ever be changing for the better.

You do literally wear your predominant order of thought in your flesh. As your spirit acts on your body it sends the elements it has absorbed from its peculiar sphere all over your body, and these elements materialize or crystallize themselves out of unseen into seen element of flesh in a manner analagous to that in which metal dissolved and invisible in a clear solution is attracted and becomes visible on the slip of copper, lead or zinc placed in such solution, or as a tree materializes leaf and fruit from unseen elements in the air about it.

But if from year to year you live in any rut of error, you add to the body an element or materialization of error in the physical. That, in other words, is sin. The proofs of sin are always decay, disease, death and physical or mental pain.

Be the spirit as crude or on as low a realm of thought as it may, yet its tendency is always upward. It brings to the body in its sleep existence a little of the more refined and powerful thought element, mixed often with a great deal of the relatively lower element of weakness. The person whose body lives till the age of eighty or ninety has a stronger spirit than the person whose body dies, say at thirty. The stronger spirit is ever demanding strength, though, perhaps, hardly conscious that it does so. That demand is in its mind when the body goes to sleep. That demand works while the body is asleep. It brings a certain amount of life to the body, but life which thus far in the history of our race has been largely adulterated with error and false belief.

But as the strong spirit does so prolong its physical life, or in other words, holds its body, then with more knowledge the spirit will grow stronger and hold a vigorous physical life much longer.

The principal error and eventual destroyer of the body's life in the case of the person aged eighty or ninety has been that person thought that the body MUST die at or near that age. The thought and opinion of all about that person seconds such idea and pushes the force of "must" in the wrong direction. "Must" is most powerful either as a destroyer or rebuilder.

After entertaining for a time the idea that decay is not an absolute necessity, proofs will come to you of its truth. True, you may have periods of prostration and weakness. Those are efforts of the new spirit or thought brought you to throw off the old elements which have so long cumbered you. But the general tendency from year to year will be **toward** better health and increase of vigor. Such has been my experience. It is now five years since I began entering on what I may call a relatively intelligent realization and experience of this order of thought. My health was never so good. I am fifty-five years of age, and my body seems almost made over anew.

The prayer or demand in the morning for the day or physical life should be to the Supreme Power for aid to help us to absorb of the best of the life or spirit of the physical world. That life is a part of the spirit of Infinite Good, or God. The growing tree, the wind, the clouds, the ocean, the river, the brook, the tiny blade of grass, the sun, the stars, are all filled with this life.

What we see or feel of these is not all of these. It is only a part, or their physical expression. Behind them and unfelt of physical sense is another life, an element, a mystery, a spirit which impels, moves and grows them.

Our minds have the marvelous capacity of drawing to themselves this life and power. Once so drawn and it remains for eternity. When you see a live tree, think or ask for the life of that tree and you will get it. When you see a flower, ask for its beauty. When you see the ocean, ask for its force. When you see anything alive that is healthful, symmetrical and well proportioned, ask for that health, symmetry and proportion. God or the Supreme Power enters into all these. They are parts of that Power. That Power or Spirit is nowhere outside of the visible or invisible universe. That

Power moves and acts in countless ways. It is in every shade of light and color cast on sea and sky. When you set your mind for a second on any one of these myriads of God's physical expressions you are communing with God, drawing nearer and nearer to that Power, making it more and more a part of yourself, and bringing to you of the peculiar quality or power, or beauty, or health, or vigor expressed in that physical thing.

While the physical senses are active by day, they can, if so directed, draw of these things. No business need be so absorbing but that a second can be so employed. That second draws some force to you.

During sleep the physical senses do not so draw. Yet the strength so drawn during the waking hours remains. It is then a help to your spirit to push its way farther into the world unseen of the physical eye and gather of the best of that world. Each day the mind being so directed adds to that strength. The higher the spirit is so pushed upward the finer and more powerful is the element absorbed by the spirit to feed the body and recuperate with more and more power the physical senses.

So body and spirit mutually act, react, and feed each other. The body is as the root of the tree. The spirit as its leaves and branches. The root draws from the earth element and force to sustain trunk, branch, leaf, blossom and fruit. Leaf and branch draws from the air an element or spirit without which trunk and root will die.

Your spirit rightly directed draws like leaf and twig element from above necessary for the body's waking existence. The body, as the root, by the help of this finer element draws from below a sustaining force for the spirit, and your other or spiritual existence.

In this manner, in ages long past, did some "walk with God," as recorded in the Old Testament, and as a result, not only were their physical lives prolonged to periods now by many deemed fabulous, as in the cases of Adam, Seth, Canain, Mahalabel, Jael and Methuselah, all of whom lived over 900 years, but some escaped physical death altogether. Because that age for some was one of greater spirituality than in ages succeeding. Greater spirituality implies a greater power for the spirit to hold and renew the physical body.

In the sixth chapter of Genesis, third verse, we read: "And the Lord said, 'My spirit shall not always strive with man for that he also is flesh; yet his days shall be an hundred and twenty years."

Many centuries after this it was written that man's limit was three score and ten, because man had fallen away still further from communion with the Supreme Power. In other words, man relied more and more on material helps and less on spiritual. This cut his physical life short. It gave the Spirit of Infinite Good less and less opportunity to "strive with man," or, in other words, act on him, spiritualize him and place him above all harm and pain from physical causes.

Of Enoch we read in Genesis, 5th chapter, 23d and 24th verses: "All the days of Enoch were 365 years. And Enoch walked with God. And he was not. For God took him."

Enoch's was a relatively perfect life. His spirit had so far dominated the physical as to cause a dematerialization of his physical body, so that it vanished from the physical eyes about him, in the same manner as did a few others mentioned in the Biblical records. As the spiritualization of our race increases (as it will increase) such dematerializations will take the place of the death of the physical body.

If you suffer from sleeplessness, it will be a help to you to say to yourself early in the day: "I am going to sleep to-night; I must sleep; I demand of the Supreme Power help to sleep."

Then you are making the spiritual conditions during the physical life of that day to draw to you elements of rest at night. When so you set your mind early in the day, you have the day's rising tide of spiritual force to assist you. For all things in nature and the natural and healthy order of life are stronger when the earth is turning toward the sun than when it is turning away from it.

Try this from day to day. Do not be discouraged if at first it does not succeed.

Try not to carry your business to bed with you. Think of rest and sleep when you retire. Some active minds so soon as their heads touch the pillow commence working, planning, fancying, speculating, wandering or worrying more vigorously than ever. An hour so spent actually makes the flesh ache through weariness. This comes of habit unconsciously acquired. The mind has become inverted, turned in the direction directly opposite from the natural way. It insists on living then in the physical, when it should be in the spiritual. It goes then into the same realm of restlessness when the body does become unconscious and feeds the body only with the elements of restlessness and weariness.

If possible change your room when you suffer from a succession of sleepless nights; change if you can temporarily your place of residence. Change often breaks the "spell" of sleeplessness. A "spell" is a web of thought woven about you and connected with the material things about you, so that when your sight or touch senses the walls, the furniture, or other articles in a room, you have sent you directly the same monotonous, unvarying set of ideas which are associated with these things. Change of physical surroundings may break this web or "spell."

If you awake at a certain hour, say one or four o'clock, for several nights in succession, don't let the idea fasten on you that you must the next night wake at that hour. Reverse this action of your mind and current of thought. Say, "I must sleep through the time." Don't let that miserable idea that your sleep must be so broken rule you. Make up your mind that you will rule it and that your real self, your spirit, shall rule your body.

If there is another person in the house who is similarly wakeful, and with whom you are in any degree of sympathy, you are liable to awake as they do through the action of their mind on yours. In such case you must either remove from their immediate presence or induce them to set their mind in the same current as yours.

Set your mind on having restful elements about you. A cat sleeping in your room or in your house two-thirds of the time is a far better aid in bringing you restful element than a nervous, restless person who must ever be moving for mere sake of moving.

Besides, the animal absorbs from you restless or sickly element and carries it off. For this reason it is healthful to have young, vigorous, harmless animals about you, but not animals or birds that are caged and deprived of liberty. The free animal kindly treated absorbs elements from you that you are continually throwing off, and which but for them you might to your hurt absorb back again. The element they so absorb from you does them no harm.

There is a suggestion of the working of this law in the "scapegoat," which yearly was loaded with the sins of the ancient Jewish people and then driven off into the wilderness.

If you have fallen into the unhealthful habit of taking narcotics, or any drug, to induce sleep, and cannot immediately break off, say in mind every time you take them: "I demand of the Supreme Power that I may be rid of the necessity of taking this artificial help as soon as possible. I demand that this drug, though it be a rotten reed to lean upon, shall help to push my spirit upward into the realms of pure and powerful thought. I demand, also, to be freed from the injurious idea that I cannot break off this habit, or that this help, imperfect as it is, cannot be made for a time a help, instead of an injury.

A drug does you far more injury when your only thought on taking it is, in substance, this: "I expect this will ruin my health, but I must have it," than when you set your mind in the condition we endeavor to indicate above.

With God "all things" are possible.

All things can be made helpful until you grow out of the necessity for their use, provided that you use or take them in the proper condition of mind or spirit, and whenever you take them you ask to get the greatest good out of them, the least of evil, and that you be freed as soon as possible from the unhealthy and unnatural condition, partly of body, but much more of mind, which their long usage may have caused you.

THE CHURCH OF SILENT DEMAND

COPYRIGHT, 1889, BY F. J. NEEDHAM.

THERE will be built in time an edifice partaking of the nature of a church, where all persons of whatever condition, age, nationality or creed may come to lay their needs before the Great Supreme Power, and demand of that Power help to supply those needs. It should be a church without sect or creed. It should be open every day during the week and every evening until a reasonable hour. It should be attended to materially and kept free from disturbance or disrespectful intrusion by some person or persons who are in sympathy with this order of thought who would accept the office as a sacred and loving trust, and for which they should receive proper compensation. It should be a place of silence for the purpose of silent demand or prayer. All who enter it for any purpose should be asked to refrain from loud talking or irreverent whispering. All who enter it should be reminded not to bring with them any frivolous mind or thought. It should be a place of earnest demand for permanent good, yet not a place of gloom or sadness.

A church should be held as a place for the concentration of the strongest thought power. The strongest thought power is that where the motive is the highest. The highest motive comes of the desire to benefit first ourselves in order to benefit others. You must have power yourself before you can help others. You can get such power by unceasing silent demand of the Supreme Power of which you are a part. You may get it the quicker through an occasional resort to a place like this chapel, which will be devoted wholly to silent demand or prayer to the Supreme Power.

Beyond the highest "ministering spirits," beyond all personal intelligence of the greatest conceivable intellect, there is a Power which pervades endless Universe. It cannot be held as within the limitations of a personality, for personality must have metes and bounds. It moves the planets in their orbits. It impels suns to give forth light and heat. It is as mysterious, incomprehensible and unexplainable in bringing the material expression of life from the tiniest seed placed in the ground, as it is in regulating the intricate movements of innumerable planetary systems. Men sometimes call it the "First Great Cause," which they have never been able to discover. It works in silence. It is the Great Supreme Power, the Spirit of Infinite Good. It is impossible, and probably ever will be, to explain its workings, for so soon as one mystery is made clear a deeper one appears behind it.

But this we do know. This Power will respond to every demand we make upon it. For we are parts of it—parts of an Infinite life, and as you a part recognize this your relationship to the Supreme Power, you will come to know that yours is the right to demand as much as possible of this Supreme or Divine Power to be expressed through you. You are a part of God "made manifest in the flesh," and it is your business to draw to you every attribute and quality that you can conceive of Deity. You want to be fearless. You want perfect health. You want complete control of appetite. You may want to be eloquent. You may want power to be pleasing others. You may want power to do business on a just, righteous and, therefore, successful basis. You may want power to cease from ugly thoughts. You may want power to rid yourself of a mind which sees only the discouraging and gloomy side in everything. You need many other qualities of character, and to gain, improve and increase these you have but to ask persistently of the Supreme Power and it shall be given you—to knock imperiously at its door, and it shall be opened unto you in time.

The victim of alcoholic excess could here have the immoderate appetite put under more control. So could the victim of hasty temper. So could the victim of a hurried mind. God is repose. Repose is power. A place dedicated to repose will give you repose, and nothing is more needed in this age of hurry and frantic effort.

The woman ostracised by society, and the man not ostracised, but both on an equality in the committal of the same sin and injury to their spirits, could here make silent demand to be led into purer lives.

Every one who enters the chapel dedicated to this Power should carry this thought with them and leave it there. "I demand of the Supreme Power good for myself. I demand of it greater health of body. I demand more clearness of mind. I demand power to rid myself of hatred, envy, jealousy and ill will toward others, for I know such thoughts or forces hurt me. I demand wisdom so that ways and means may come to me to get health of body, clearness of mind, and freedom from the bondage of evil thought toward others. Lastly, I wish to leave here a thought which may benefit others who come here. If they are in physical pain, let it be ceased. If they are weak and lame or sick, or in any way afflicted, I demand that I draw from the highest, and leave here my quota of power to help them and cure them. If any come here in trouble of mind, let me leave my little to relieve that, for I know that if I leave here some force to so help others, that force will come back to me tenfold in time. It is as bread I cast upon the waters to return after many days."

If all who enter or use a room unite in putting out the same kind of thought while there, they charge or fill that room with that order of thought. If it is the thought of power and help, it will leave in that room the spirit and force of power and help. If hundreds or thousands come *in such spirit* to that place or church, each will leave his or her quota of power and help there. The result will be the storing, and constant accumulation of an immense force for good in that chapel, presuming it be never used for other purposes, and that lower, worldly, sordid and selfish thought be kept out of it.

The force so left will assist greatly in healing those sick in body who come and demand in faith; it will strengthen the weak spirit; it will give comfort and cheer to those in affliction. Five minutes spent in this chapel of Silent Demand may do you great good.

Some of our churches are to-day unconsciously desecrated. People enter, bringing all their worldly thought with them. They may not have, on entering, a silent wish that such thought be left behind. They whisper to each other fragments of social and worldly matters; they look over the congregation with the mind of curiosity or the mind centered on the apparel and ornamentation of others. Long conversations sometimes occur before service near the doors. After service there is sometimes lingering in the body of the church and light conversation on subjects entirely foreign to the nature and real use of that place. There is sometimes no reverence whatever for the church when service is not being held. If called there on any business or service people are allowed to talk and act as they would in the street or corner grocery. Fairs, concerts, exhibitions and other public performances are sometimes held in the body of the church.

All this leaves its order of thought in the church.

There is not always an effort to bring a mood into the church appropriate to a place where the ruling thought should be that of a serious, earnest demand to draw nigh and be connected in thought with the Supreme Power of Infinite Good, eternal and incomprehensible, which, knowing neither time nor space, rules the eternity of Universe. We can draw to us more and more of this power, become more and more a part of it and be one with the spirit of Infinite Good. We need in the church, more than in any other place, to feel the majesty, dignity and sublimity of the Supreme Power as a spirit brooding over that place. Then we could go forth literally bathed, refreshed and strengthened in spirit, and when out of the sacred portals, laugh and sing, be filled with mirth and cheerfulness, and enjoy all that life gives for enjoyment.

Then those who come to pray, or demand relief from physical or mental suffering, would, if coming in the spirit of good-will to all, receive of such relief and at the same time leave some of their power for the relief of others.

Such a church—indeed a system of such churches dedicated to silent prayer of the Supreme Power is needed all over the land, because thousands in their homes have little or no privacy where they can withdraw even for a few moments, in order to connect themselves with a higher current of thought. Their rooms may be liable to intrusion at any moment. A place liable to intrusive interruption at any moment is already spiritually intruded upon.

Again, the spirit or thought left in their rooms is not favorable for the quickest answer to the prayer of earnest demand. Too much mind has been in it, and may be ever going in it, giving out peevishness, selfishness, envy and other evil thought, with not a shadow of desire for relief from such thought. Such thought is left in the room and makes it the more difficult for the earnest mind to lift itself above it.

We use the term "above it" in its most literal sense. The lower or more material thought is a real element. It is a real stratum or cloud of denser element or thought which is an obstacle to the entrance and effect on our minds of the higher and more elevated element of thought. The higher can never be prevented ultimately from piercing this denser thought atmosphere, and coming to us to give us strength and lift us up in every way. But the higher power can be retarded and delayed in coming to us. Certain material conditions can help the higher thought to come and act on us more quickly than if not granted.

Of these the chapel in question would be one. It would be a place which, when properly kept, would retain only the higher power of thought. As we have said in a previous number, a room becomes filled and saturated with whatever order of thought, mood of mind or purpose that is most in it, and such thought so left exerts its power on all who enter that room, especially those who enter with similar mood of mind and purpose. If a chapel then is dedicated and used only as a place for the mood of silent aspiration, the element of aspiration would more and more fill such place. Into that you could enter, and be literally bathed in a purer and stronger thought atmosphere. You would, as coming in with desire to better yourself and others, leave also an element to better others even as the element left by others in like desire will benefit you. If harassed by the worry, disturbance and bustle of your home, you go to our chapel and demand rest, peace of mind and renewed strength, which may even turn your trials to pleasures, you will, when in the right mind, leave some of the power you draw down to benefit others coming after you. If afflicted in body you will, when demanding in that frame of mind, draw also power to heal yourself and likewise leave power to heal others. For it is a law of nature that you cannot be really and permanently benefited yourself without benefiting others. Every "perfect gift" is a gift not sent to you only, but to others. A "perfect gift" must come from the Supreme Power, or, in other words, the "Spirit of Infinite Good." Our demand from that power must always be tempered with a willingness on our part to defer to its wisdom. If we will defer to that wisdom—if we, in mind, say in our prayer, "I want some particular thing very much, but if a wisdom greater than mine sees that it is not good for me in the shape I want it, then I will not demand it;" we shall in time receive a perfect good, and a good which will come to stay. But if we will not so defer but say and pray in this spirit, "I want what I demand anyway, I defer to no higher wisdom; I don't care if what I want is an injustice to others or not," then we shall in time still receive what we desire, if persistent in that desire or prayer. But it will prove an imperfect gift and a one-sided pleasure, with more of the bitter than the sweet—as much a curse as a blessing—a gift with which we must part in time, so great will be the trouble or pain inflicted by it.

In such spirit do people constantly pray for money, and money only. They get money in accordance with the law, but how often at the cost of health, of life, or of all ability to enjoy anything save the mere getting of money. But when we pray for money in accordance with the WHOLE law, we shall get it and every other blessing with it. Then we receive a "perfect gift."

The prompting or impulse of our spirit to make some material acknowledgment or donation for aid received should never be choked off. When you throw your penny, or whatever you feel you can reasonably give into the poor box, you are, if giving wholly in the spirit of good intent to all, bestowing much more than the material coin. A thought or force of aid goes with that piece of money. This thought needs something material in order to give it more power to work on the material stratum of life. Material gifts do carry with them the thought or mood of the givers, and when you handle or wear such gifts you will draw from them of that thought or mood. A ring or any article of jewelry, if given another in a churlish or grudging spirit, or because it is extorted or indirectly begged, carries with it an evil thought, and connects also the person who wears it with the same current of grudging thought as it flows from the giver. But if the ring or other article is given in the spirit of hearty good-will, it brings with it the beneficial thought current of good will from the giver. In this manner are material presents in a sense the actual mediums or conveyances of beneficial or injurious thoughts from giver to receiver.

"It is better to give than to receive," said the Christ of Judea. Because when things are given from the impulse of hearty good-will, the one who gives actually receives in the thought element of good wishes from the one who receives a constant flow back of beneficial thought every time the one who takes is reminded of the gift. You give a ring in this spirit. You forget for long periods that ever you gave it. But every time the one who wears that ring looks at it, he or she is reminded of you, and with that reminder you receive a heart throb of loving remembrance. This brings to you from the wearer a constant flow or pulsation of good-will which is for you life and force.

Boxes for offerings or donations in money should be placed in this chapel, so that those who feel an impulse to give in hearty spirit of good-will should have opportunity to do so. But nothing should go into those boxes unless the giver *feels* a live pleasure in giving. No grudging thought accompanying a piece of money is wanted in that chapel.

Such a thought adulterates and weakens the power for good stored in that place.

We ask of every reader of the WHITE CROSS LIBRARY an earnest thought or desire for the building of such a chapel. Every such thought is a prayer and a force working to build it. Many such prayers coming from different minds and focussed on one purpose, will build it. If an impulse to give any sum of money, no matter how small, towards its erection is felt, let it follow the thought. But let it here be thoroughly understood that we rely altogether on the spiritual power coming of the prayers or demands of those in hearty accord with this special purpose. So that your prayer or demand is in the right spirit, the material means for building this chapel are sure to follow from the impulses of yours and other's spirits.

The guardian of such a chapel will be in entire sympathy with its spirit and purpose. That guardian should be a woman, for the feminine mind and organization first receives of the Supreme Power in thought and force. The feminine influence, power and care should predominate in such a place. This guardianship and care of the chapel will be received as a sacred and loving trust. No woman will take it merely for the money it brings her. Her whole heart will be in this office. It will be a position as sacred and important as that of minister or priest. For to her is committed the responsibility of keeping pure the thought atmosphere of the chapel, in other words the ordering and supervision of all its physical requirements, so that the entrance of the Supreme Power and its beneficial action on those who come to get relief shall be retarded as little as possible.

The purer, the more devotional the thought atmosphere of such a chapel is kept, the freer it is from flippant or sordid thought, the greater the opportunities will be afforded for the entrance to it of "ministering spirits" of the highest order. You can create a thought atmosphere which will serve as a literal channel to a room or chapel for powerful and benevolent mind unseen of the physical eye to enter. On the contrary, if your thought and the thought of others in any room or place is entirely of a vulgar, ugly, dishonest or low character, there is created thereby a literal means of communication to you and that place for the same class of evil mind.

When donations are received for the purpose of building this chapel, they can be sent to our office in New York. They will be placed in some bank as a deposit for a sacred purpose, and so held and kept. It matters not how small the donation so that the right spirit accompany it. That spirit more than the coin is the force which will build many chapels consecrated to Silent Demand of the Supreme Power.

We can give no other pledge or security for faithfully using the money so sent for the purpose here stated, than in the feeling we may inspire in your hearts that we are and shall be earnest, sincere and honest in carrying out this purpose. Our accountability for ourself and the Spirit of Infinite Good is far more potent to keep us from doing evil than any pledge or security we can give you.

It may be two, five, seven or more years before such chapel be built. It may be sooner. Like everything else it must be built spiritually before it is physically. Railroads, ships, houses, all of man's physical accomplishments, are built first in mind ere they appear in wood, stone or iron. The Chapel of Silent Demand is here built, spiritually, in this book. Its material correspondence in wood and stone will follow more or less quickly according to the degree of faith and live belief of this age and generation in the actual reality of the Supreme Power, and the greater good which would come of a working, living faith in this grand reality.

If the city of New York is the best place for the first Chapel of Silent Demand to be built, it will be in New York. If some other city holds more of the live and working faith in these truths, it will be built in that city.

The building need not be very large nor costly. Elegance, simplicity and dignity need not involve great expense.

We suggest the following inscription as appropriate to be placed on the front of the chapel:

"THE CHURCH OF SILENT PRAYER

TO

THE SUPREME POWER."

And the following placed so as to be clearly read within the chapel:

"Demand first wisdom so as to know what to ask for."

"Ask and ye shall receive. Ask imperiously, but ask in a willing mood for what the Supreme Power sees best for you."

"Love thy neighbor as thyself, but demand good first for yourself that you may be the better fitted to do good to all."

I have spoken here not as a person, but only as the enunciator of a principle. It matters little whether I or others are directly concerned in the material erection of a Church of Silent Demand. It is the principle, not the personality, that we seek to establish. But when this principle is materially recognized and put in force through the building of but one such church, and that church is put and kept in the right hands to favor silent prayer and the concentration of the higher thought and divine force, the results in the healing of sick bodies, and, above all, the healing of the sick spirits behind those bodies will be greater than has been seen in this and many preceding ages.

PRENTICE MULFORD.

BOOK JUNGLE

Bringing Classics to Life
www.bookjungle.com email: sales@bookjungle.com fax: 630-214-0564 mail: Book Jungle PO Box 2226 Champaign, IL 61825

QTY

The Two Babylons
Alexander Hislop
You may be surprised to learn that many traditions of Roman Catholicism in fact don't come from Christ's teachings but from an ancient Babylonian "Mystery" religion that was centered on Nimrod, his wife Semiramis, and a child Tammuz. This book shows how this ancient religion transformed itself as it incorporated Christ into its teachings....

Religion/History Pages:358
ISBN: *1-59462-010-5*   MSRP *$22.95*

The Power Of Concentration
Theron Q. Dumont
It is of the utmost value to learn how to concentrate. To make the greatest success of anything you must be able to concentrate your entire thought upon the idea you are working on. The person that is able to concentrate utilizes all constructive thoughts and shuts out all destructive ones...

Self Help/Inspirational   Pages:196
ISBN: *1-59462-141-1*   MSRP *$14.95*

Rightly Dividing The Word
Clarence Larkin
The "Fundamental Doctrines" of the Christian Faith are clearly outlined in numerous books on Theology, but they are not available to the average reader and were mainly written for students. The Author has made it the work of his ministry to preach the "Fundamental Doctrines." To this end he has aimed to express them in the simplest and clearest manner..

Religion   Pages:352
ISBN: *1-59462-334-1*   MSRP *$23.45*

The Law of Psychic Phenomena
Thomson Jay Hudson
"I do not expect this book to stand upon its literary merits; for if it is unsound in principle, felicity of diction cannot save it, and if sound, homeliness of expression cannot destroy it. My primary object in offering it to the public is to assist in bringing Psychology within the domain of the exact sciences. That this has never been accomplished..."

New Age   Pages:420
ISBN: *1-59462-124-1*   MSRP *$29.95*

Beautiful Joe
Marshall Saunders
When Marshall visited the Moore family in 1892, she discovered Joe, a dog they had nursed back to health from his previous abusive home to live a happy life. So moved was she, that she wrote this classic masterpiece which won accolades and was recognized as a heartwarming symbol for humane animal treatment...

Fiction   Pages:256
ISBN: *1-59462-261-2*   MSRP *$18.45*

Bringing Classics to Life

BOOK JUNGLE

www.bookjungle.com email: sales@bookjungle.com fax: 630-214-0564 mail: Book Jungle PO Box 2226 Champaign, IL 61825

The Go-Getter
Kyne B. Peter

QTY

The Go Getter is the story of William Peck. He was a war veteran and amputee who will not be refused what he wants. Peck not only fights to find employment but continually proves himself more than competent at the many difficult test that are throw his way in the course of his early days with the Ricks Lumber Company...

Business/Self Help/Inspirational   Pages: 68

ISBN: *1-59462-186-1*   *MSRP* *$8.95*

Self Mastery
Emile Coue

Emile Coue came up with novel way to improve the lives of people. He was a pharmacist by trade and often saw ailing people. This lead him to develop autosuggestion, a form of self-hypnosis. At the time his theories weren't popular but over the years evidence is mounting that he was indeed right all along...

New Age/Self Help   Pages: 98

ISBN: *1-59462-189-6*   *MSRP* *$7.95*

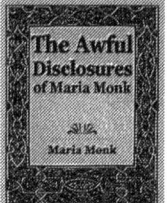

The Awful Disclosures Of Maria Monk

"I cannot banish the scenes and characters of this book from my memory. To me it can never appear like an amusing fable, or lose its interest and importance. The story is one which is continually before me, and must return fresh to my mind with painful emotions as long as I live..."

Religion   Pages: 232

ISBN: *1-59462-160-8*   *MSRP* *$17.95*

As a Man Thinketh
James Allen

"This little volume (the result of meditation and experience) is not intended as an exhaustive treatise on the much-written-upon subject of the power of thought. It is suggestive rather than explanatory, its object being to stimulate men and women to the discovery and perception of the truth that by virtue of the thoughts which they choose and encourage..."

Inspirational/Self Help   Pages: 80

ISBN: *1-59462-231-0*   *MSRP* *$9.45*

The Enchanted April
Elizabeth Von Arnim

It began in a woman's club in London on a February afternoon, an uncomfortable club, and a miserable afternoon when Mrs. Wilkins, who had come down from Hampstead to shop and had lunched at her club, took up The Times from the table in the smoking-room...

Fiction   Pages: 368

ISBN: *1-59462-150-0*   *MSRP* *$23.45*

Bringing Classics to Life

BOOK JUNGLE

www.bookjungle.com email: sales@bookjungle.com fax: 630-214-0564 mail: Book Jungle PO Box 2226 Champaign, IL 61825

The Codes Of Hammurabi And Moses - W. W. Davies

The discovery of the Hammurabi Code is one of the greatest achievements of archaeology, and is of paramount interest, not only to the student of the Bible, but also to all those interested in ancient history...

Religion   Pages:132
ISBN: *1-59462-338-4*   MSRP *$12.95*

The Thirty-Six Dramatic Situations
Georges Polti

An incredibly useful guide for aspiring authors and playwrights. This volume categorizes every dramatic situation which could occur in a story and describes them in a list of 36 situations. A great aid to help inspire or formalize the creative writing process...

Self Help/Reference   Pages:204
ISBN: *1-59462-134-9*   MSRP *$15.95*

Holland - The History Of Netherlands
Thomas Colley Grattan

Thomas Grattan was a prestigious writer from Dublin who served as British Consul to the US. Among his works is an authoritative look at the history of Holland. A colorful and interesting look at history....

History/Politics   Pages:408
ISBN: *1-59462-137-3*   MSRP *$26.95*

A Concise Dictionary of Middle English
A. L. Mayhew
Walter W. Skeat

The present work is intended to meet, in some measure, the requirements of those who wish to make some study of Middle-English, and who find a difficulty in obtaining such assistance as will enable them to find out the meanings and etymologies of the words most essential to their purpose...

Reference/History   Pages:332
ISBN: *1-59462-119-5*   MSRP *$29.95*

The Witch-Cult in Western Europe
Margaret Murray

QTY

The mass of existing material on this subject is so great that I have not attempted to make a survey of the whole of European "Witchcraft" but have confined myself to an intensive study of the cult in Great Britain. In order, however, to obtain a clearer understanding of the ritual and beliefs I have had recourse to French and Flemish sources...

Occult   Pages:308
ISBN: *1-59462-126-8*   MSRP *$22.45*

Bringing Classics to Life

BOOK JUNGLE

www.bookjungle.com *email:* sales@bookjungle.com *fax:* 630-214-0564 *mail:* Book Jungle PO Box 2226 Champaign, IL 61825

Name	
Email	
Telephone	
Address	
City, State ZIP	

☐ **Credit Card** ☐ **Check / Money Order**

Credit Card Number	
Expiration Date	
Signature	

Please Mail to: Book Jungle
　　　　　　　　PO Box 2226
　　　　　　　　Champaign, IL 61825
or Fax to: 　　　630-214-0564

ORDERING INFORMATION

web: *www.bookjungle.com*
email: *sales@bookjungle.com*
fax: *630-214-0564*
mail: *Book Jungle PO Box 2226 Champaign, IL 61825*
or PayPal *to sales@bookjungle.com*

Please contact us for bulk discounts
DIRECT-ORDER TERMS

**20% Discount if You Order
Two or More Books**
Free Domestic Shipping!

www.ingramcontent.com/pod-product-compliance
Lightning Source LLC
Chambersburg PA
CBHW080503110426
42742CB00017B/2987